THE RESULTS MAP FOR WOMEN IN BIZ

KIMBERLY ALEXANDER

MOTIVATING
THE MASSES
—PRESS—

Published by Motivating the Masses Press, Inc.
7777 N Wickham Rd, # 12-247
Melbourne, FL 32940
www.MotivationalPress.com

Manufactured in the United States of America.

ISBN: 978-1-62865-224-6

CONTENTS

———————

DEDICATION

_____

For my Mom

My hero, who taught me that strength,
courage and beauty start from within.

For my daughters, Emma and Megan

You inspire me every day to be the best woman I can be and to put that
strength, courage and beauty to good use, just as you do.

FOREWORD

Michelle Jones
President, Lulu Avenue

Congratulations, you clearly are looking to make a change in your life because you have in your hands The Results Map for Women in Biz, written by my dear friend, Strategist and Mentor Kimberly Alexander. I remember the first time I met Kimberly, my boss at the time was excited about this new hire she had made and had asked me to meet with her. She wanted me to be her mentor as she was on boarded into our business. Kimberly was a breath of fresh air, bright, bubbly and full of ideas and enthusiasm for her new adventure. We chatted for a few minutes and I went about my business for the day. I never realized that day was the beginning of a very special bond and relationship that would last a lifetime.

The next time I encountered Kimberly was at a training event I had to attend, kicking and screaming I might add! Here, I met Kimberly once again and we quickly realized we had a connection, and it wasn't just the red wine! I spent many hours connecting with Kimberly that week, learning about her passions and what drove her. I quickly realized that Kimberly was a very special lady, destined to channel her knowledge and energy into empowering women to achieve what matters most in their lives and to build amazing businesses.

Often times particularly for us women, we don't spend enough time focused on our own self development. Many of us have short and long term goals, dreams and aspirations. Without a plan it's hard to accomplish what is most important in our lives. The Results Map for Women in Biz that Kimberly has created is the tool I believe every woman needs. The Results Map helps you discover what is most important in your life and business right now and then helps guide you to establish a plan to get you where you want to be. You have all heard the saying, "If you don't plan, you plan to fail." It's so true. Planning what you need to do in order to accomplish your goals and dreams is vital to you successfully moving toward for what matters most to you. Planning really is the difference between success and failure.

Kimberly and The Results Map for Women in Biz has made a huge impact on how I live my life day to day and how I achieve what matters most. Let The Results Map for Women in Biz be your guide as you take valuable time investing in yourself, your future, and to achieve what matters most to you.

Good Luck!

Executive Summary

The Results Map is a comprehensive, how-to system to identify what you want to achieve within your biz and life, and how to go after it. Exercises and action steps will guide you on how to get it. You will be taking action to move through your map, beginning at the starting point, and then working through your journey with the end result, discovering your hidden treasure: your results.

You may discover challenges along the way, taking a wrong turn, skipping over steps and even stumbling or falling here and there. Get back up and brush yourself off. Follow the proven process that has helped over hundreds of female entrepreneurs, executives and leaders navigate through their journey to find the results they have been searching for.

Chapter 1: The Starting Point

In Chapter One you will gain a clear understanding of the three fundamentals of The Results Map: perspective, strategy, and results and why they are important in your journey.

Chapter 2: Fear of the Horizon

In Chapter Two, learn steps to take action while leaving emotion out of the process. Learn why you hold onto fear and how to overcome it. Often enough, tough choices come with making changes. Allow yourself to open up to new ideas and strategies. Understanding your fears and how they impact your choices in your biz and life are a critical step in taking the right actions.

Chapter 3: Heavy Weight

We all have a past, and often times it can hinder the future. In Chapter Three, take a different perspective on how heavy weight from your past matters and is necessary to embrace for the journey of who you are intended to become. This chapter will teach you how to learn the lessons while ditching the heavy weight, allowing you to grow past your potential and see new possibilities.

Chapter 4: Get Clear

In Chapter Four you will identify your purpose and next steps to take in your journey. How do you embrace it and what the heck do you do with it? Identify what your purpose is, and to whom would you love to serve. Learn how to identify the knowledge you will need to build your biz quicker and with the right supports.

Chapter 5: You're Crew

It is almost impossible to embark on any journey without a crew; your team of people will help you get to where you plan to go and have your back every step of the way. In Chapter Five, learn how to find the right team and get them on board to put your plans in motion through the Four I's: Identify, Inspire, Influence, and Impact. If you envision trudging through the map on your own, you will not find your treasure. It takes a team to reach the destination.

Chapter 6: The Destination

Now at base camp, you cannot head up the hill unless you understand the plan. In Chapter Six, you will identify and understand what you want to accomplish both professionally and personally. When identifying your planned accomplishments you will ask yourself three questions: Does it make a positive impact on my biz and life? Does it make me proud? Without it, would I be fulfilled? Identifying "what" you want and "why" you want it will be your driver. The "when" and "who" will get you there. There are simple, yet intensive exercises that must be completed before you take your first step on your journey.

Chapter 7: Chart your course

Fasten your harness, you are headed straight up the mountain! In Chapter Seven you will learn how to chart your course and set your strategy. This can be an uphill climb, but the view at the top will be worth it. You will identify what tasks will move you forward, and what tasks will set you back. By identifying your non-negotiable activities you will be able to strategically "get real" with the time needed to achieve your planned accomplishments.

Chapter 8: Defining those Boundaries

In Chapter Eight you will learn steps to set boundaries; a critical element to your Results Map. Even if you have the best plan and people in place, if you don't have the right amount of time assigned to it, will you realistically be able to achieve what you set out to do? In this chapter you will work through exercises to learn how to mirror your time with your planned accomplishments.

Chapter 9: Getting it Done

Another mountain to climb, but you are gaining ground to reach the peak. In Chapter Nine, learn about setting systems in place to get results. Systems are the key to effectiveness, keeping your map intact, and driving the results you're searching for.

Chapter 10: All In

Chapter Ten is when you are ready to cross the bridge from reactionary to proactive. You are ready to put your Results Map into action, which can take great discipline and continuous influence. In this chapter you will cross-check all that you have learned to ensure that every system is in sync and always with the principle of mirroring your time to your planned accomplishments.

Chapter 11: Onward

Congratulations! You have reached the peak. Changing behaviors can be dramatic and even though your plan and action steps are in place, you may still slip into old habits. Stay on course and spot-check your progress and results. You may need to make tweaks along the way. Chapter Eleven will guide you through making changes for the better and for long term growth.

Your journey awaits...

Chapter 1
The Starting Point

_____

"Sometimes, it takes a specific event to wake you up!"
-Rebecca Barth

Ladies, the time has come to get to the heart of the matter. Life is hard…Period. This constant struggle of striving for success in every area of our lives is a bit, well, exhausting. As women, we tend to feel this need to own everything from the household, to our business, and to volunteering our time. We give 150% of ourselves with nothing left but to fall into bed at the end of the day and do it all over again in the morning.

What is up with that?

Well my fellow fabulous women who do the biz thing, the family thing, the friend thing, the volunteer thing, the everything-thing, here is a map of how to live a life of challenge, determination, success, self-fulfillment and gratitude. You can do this, all while building a biz and being present in your life. We don't have a personal life or a biz life. We only have one life! Yes, life is hard, but only as hard as you choose to make it. And I must say, it is pretty amazing when you live it to your fullest potential.

It's time to get real on how you want to live it!

So, I have the solution to get you there! _The Results Map for Women in Biz_ is a series of thought-starters and exercises that will open your heart and mind, and allow you to chart a course to the business you want to build and the life you want to live. You will not find all of your answers on one page. Sisters, trust the process. What you will learn are the fundamentals needed to make smart decisions, and tweak behaviors in order to bring you the "ah-ha, oh yes" break trough's you are looking for. In this chapter, you will learn the main fundamentals of The Results Map and why they are important to building your rock star plan. Throughout the book, this fundamental learning and the exercises to follow will form your Map.

The three fundamentals are: perspective, strategy and results. In all of the decisions I make, all the plans I develop and the end result I strive for, I first walk through these steps. Moving forward, you will too. You will be able to identify how to cut the frustrations of biz and life, strategies that work, and how to double your happiness, maybe even triple it, from the results you experience.

I have a surprise for you. In every chapter you will find a story from a brave and courageous woman's journey. Some are just starting out, some are still headed towards the summit, and some have reached the peak. I included stories of struggle and success for a reason. These stories will help you see and understand that you are not alone. Being a woman in biz can be a scary and lonely place. What I want you to understand is that there are incredible gals out there that are living, breathing, laughing, and crying their way to their peak, just like you. Please read their stories. They will give you fresh perspective and a lot of inspiration that you too need to start climbing! These fabulous, and I mean absolutely fabulous, women have touched and stirred up my soul and impacted my life. I am forever grateful to all eleven of them for inviting us into their world.

One thing I can assure you, the answers you are searching for, maybe even cannot put into words yet, will be in front of you in black and white. A life in black and white, can you imagine that? Taking the drama and emotion out of making decisions for your biz and life is pretty powerful. No worries, we will add a splash of color to the mix, but in due time. What you need to promise yourself is to read every word, take the time to complete every exercise, and follow the process. Your map will form if you follow each step in order, and not one word sooner. I have personally mentored hundreds of women through this program, and it is only completely effective if you take it one step at a time. Bring the tissues; we are going to do some good work together.

Let me give you an idea about following the process. Have you ever been in a workshop or completing a home self-study course, and you fast-forward ahead? You skip steps and cannot understand why you were not seeing results? This is like opening up a brand new board game, not reading the instructions, and diving in thinking you can figure it out. It just doesn't work that way, like everything else in biz and in life,

The work brings the rewards.

I know this example was simplistic. The same is true when you are looking for answers in challenges in your biz. They are right in front of you, but you just cannot see them yet. Before you spend another dime or dream up another "build-it quick" strategy, just stop and read.

The answers lie within the perspectives, strategies and results of your map

Brilliance is waiting and it's closer than you can ever imagine. Don't you just love that? The answers are here! I am excited to see what will unfold for you.

First, let's do a little dreaming. What does your biz and team that you want, need, or envision look like? If you could have the biz of your dreams, would you make the changes to get it? Do you even know where to start? Could the results you are seeing now be elevated, enhanced, and made bigger? The difference between seeing results and dreaming of them is perspective, and the willingness to change and take action. Let's get a little uncomfortable. Wait, scratch that, and let's get a lot of uncomfortable! Being uncomfortable allows you to grow, think outside of the box, and develop past your potential.

Your quest does not start yet. First I'm going to share with you my story of how this book came to life. Reinventing my biz and life goals was a journey, and what I needed was a map to get me there. It involved changing my perspective of the purpose behind my work, and shifts into my personal strategies and my biz strategies. I decided to share the tools I developed and used to see results so that anyone could do the same. I found it a personal responsibility to share The Results Map with as many people as possible. The map you are about to build and the journey you are ready to embark on is one I took many years ago. You see, I wrote The Results Map for myself. Really, this process changed my life for the better and brought positive change. I developed this program to save my life, and sure enough, it did.

Since birth, I have been an overachiever. I am an out of the box, think big, climb to the top, can-do-more gal. I strive and drive to be the best in all that I do, from the household, to the meeting room, to the kid's activities, to the gym and the list goes on and on. Now, there have been times where this has gotten me ahead and there have been times where it was flat out unhealthy. Just because you are an over-achiever doesn't mean you always win and, often times, doesn't get you ahead. These are big lessons I have learned, and they almost cost me what matters most in my life.

I worked for a company that I absolutely loved and believed in. I put in the hours because of that belief, but more than that I had a need to make a difference. I ran through airports, gave 150% of myself 15 to 18 hours a day and put every last ounce of energy into "the job". Sadly, what I put very little into was my own personal development and life. Every ounce of energy went into building and achieving results. My incredible husband and children, my health, my family and friends, and my home took the backseat. The team that I lead started noticing a change in me that I am sure led them to disappointment and concern. The over-achiever in me was transforming into an under-achiever. Call more meetings, create more quick-win promotions, make more calls, the list goes on and on. "More, more, more" was my mantra. Sadly, it gave me less in every area of my life. The life that I had in front of me was vanishing. In a nutshell, I lost all perspective on my biz and life. I had severe foggy, tunnel vision and couldn't see what was in front of me or around me. The problem was that the results I wanted, both professionally and personally, were floundering and I was losing my sense of self. The numbers, the bottom line, and the growth forecasts were all driving everything in my life. I literally had no idea what I stood for, where I wanted to head, and who I wanted to become. Have you ever been there? It's a dark, lonely, and scary place.

One weekend I was home and very, very tired after weeks and weeks of tireless travel. I was so exhausted when I was home on the weekends, it was practically impossible to be present, let alone keep my eyes open for anything. I had fallen asleep while reading a book to my little girls on night, and I felt a little nudge on my shoulder. My daughter asked me to wake up and finish the story. I looked up and there in front of me was my husband with tears in his eyes. He told me that he missed me and asked me to come back to them. Where had I gone, I was right in front of him? Yes, physically in front of him but not mentally present. Mentally I was somewhere else.

I felt empty and helpless. I had brought my husband to tears, I couldn't give my daughters the time they deserved, and I didn't know if I was up, down, or inside out. Later that day I got on the scale and I was thirty pounds heavier. I remember trudging up the stairs every night with a glass of wine in tow, just to fall asleep. Often times I would trudge back down to get another. I felt completely lousy mentally and physically, and I didn't know what to do. Lost would be the perfect word.

One day I started asking myself, "How did I get here. Who have I become?" Is this the life I dreamed of living? Have I traded a life with my husband and children, whom I love and adore, for a life on the road? Do I have the right relationships? Am I taking care of myself to live a healthy and fulfilled life? Falling to my knees that day in anguish, I sat and reflected on previous months with my team and peers, and how hard I had started to push them, all to get the numbers. I started counting how many days I was home versus being gone and the number was staggering. I was losing sleep, crying daily, working harder, going backward and living in a reaction mode. This was a life-changing moment for me. At that moment, I decided to change my perspective, otherwise, I would simply lose everything I loved, everything I lived for, and everything that mattered to me. So that is what I did...

I changed my Perspective.

I decided to tweak my expectations of what the perfect job looked like and what it took to get results. I wanted less travel and task-oriented duties; I needed to put people first and find balance. Yes, balance. That was my dealmaker, not the money or the title, but to be present in everything I did.

No more running and no more reaction mode. Perspective and strategy were what I needed to get the job done and live a purpose-lead life.

So I asked myself, what was driving me to over-achieve? Why did I have this need to excel without regard to my needs or those of my loved ones? I needed to find a way to compromise and get the sense of professional satisfaction I wanted without damaging my health and my relationships. After all, being an over-achiever isn't bad; it's keeping that drive in check that matters.

Perspective rocks. It takes you back to the drawing board for bigger things to unfold.

So here is what I did. I cut unnecessary tasks and was streamlining my focus on my team's strengths and what needed to be accomplished. Work smarter, not harder was an understatement. I would reach out to my team on Sundays to tell them to stop working, because I knew they were. Simplistic approaches, high-level support and training, strong follow through, and more balance were the keys. And eventually my team made big numbers and I had a life too, go figure! I started seeing changes for the better. I was present in my life. With less chaos and craziness at work I was able to focus on the most important areas of my life: my family, my friends, my health, and my sense of self. It takes discipline to change and get the results you want, but with a clear, strategic plan and perspective you will get there, gals.

My story isn't anything you haven't read before. And that's the point. This story repeats itself again and again in the business community, and it's time for us gals to make a change. And that change starts with you. So many people curse the big, bad corporate world, but that world was good to me. So much so that I was in that area for over 20 years, and it made me who I am today. But to everything is a season, and the time had come for a change in my life. The Results Map gave me the steps and courage to make big changes that lead to growth and possibility.

So let's jump in and get started. As I shared earlier, the foundation of The Results Map begins with three simple, yet powerful fundamentals.

Perspective, Strategy and Results.

This book will guide you through these three fundamentals in order to plan your Results Map. From one map to the next, every woman's plan will have similarities, but will be very different. Everyone is hiking toward different goals, with varied skill sets, perspectives, demands, and even dreams. One thing to be mindful of, and I will continue to repeat this fact, is to follow the process. Don't skip over chapters. Some may shake you to the core, and that is good. Every chapter is in this book for a reason. Allow yourself the growth needed to work toward the Results Map you desire and need.

The answers lie within this book, trust me.

» Perspective will bring you self-discovery through purpose, people and whom you desire to serve.

» Strategy will put your plan, boundaries, time, and systems in place.

» Results will be driven by your actions.

» We will go deeper throughout every chapter, exploring each fundamental noted above and laying the foundation of your Results Map. As you are reading, keep a few things in mind:

» This book is not a quick fix, but a guide that will require continuous tweaks and follow up. I still take myself through The Results Map at the start of every quarter as my biz grows and evolves.

» You will be learning the strategies and tools to get you to where you want to be.

» You are working to end less productive habits and create new, effective habits. Be patient. It takes time to change.

» Change can be challenging. However, it will bring great rewards.

» Learn from your past to thrive in your present and future.

Throughout the book there will be learning, exercises and action items. Taking the steps to develop your Results Map will help you understand and achieve the outcomes in life and in biz that you want. I want to see that happen for you. Greatness awaits, just push through to get it.

See it through and don't give up.

Write, highlight, scribble, cross out and write again. Do the work and the rewards will come.

You have one blissful life to live, so make it your absolute best. Now let's get to work.

Rebecca Barth
RebeccaBarth.com

Villain: "You must pay the rent…"

Damsel: "I can't pay the rent!"

Hero: "Then I'll pay the rent!"

Damsel: "My hero!"

Villain: "Curses! Foiled again…"

And thus, with a rolled up tissue used as a villain's mustache, a damsel's hair bow, and a hero's bow tie, my speaking career began.

At three years old, family and friends cheered me on. I loved the stage and it loved me.

In first grade, and annually for several years after, I wrote, directed, and starred in school productions that I practiced during recess with my friends. We even were allowed to go to other classrooms and present the plays. My poor teachers! My poor friends! Then at age 13, I was set on becoming a lawyer, with plans for law school in my long-range goals. What happened?

Some good-natured individual had informed me that while being on stage was a great dream, I might want to think of a back-up plan, since so few people make it in that industry. And I believed her.

Fast-forward high school, college and now two years into law school; I knew I was in the wrong place. Always driven, I was getting awesome grades there. I even had the law firm I was working for paying my way! I had a job as an attorney in a corporate law firm all but waiting for me when I graduated. Everything was lined up for a perfect C-Suite life. Success. Money. Prestige. Best thing I ever did? Become a law school dropout.

Take a moment to think back to your own childhood. What did you want to do? Who did you want to be? Is the itch still there?

I followed the corporate path next, becoming an upper-level manager, and even a VP. But I was still not content. When I got that elusive VP title, I thought I would be happy. But dissatisfaction was just below the surface. I blamed it on other factors: "I'm not a COO yet." "I still am not making the money I wanted." "I haven't arrived quite yet." Meanwhile, as a "hobby," I was in various plays, joined Toastmasters, gave speeches, and as many presentations at work as possible. Need someone to talk on…well, anything? Sign me up.

Sometimes, it takes a specific event to wake you up! I can remember the specific conversation. I was asked not to use humor anymore. They wanted a more stoic, professional me. Looking back, the comment was valid for the situation—and I learned a lot about appropriate and inappropriate humor that day-- but it was a trigger point for me. It was the catalyst. I am so thankful for that conversation now, although at the time I was devastated. Without it, though, fear may have kept me from freedom.

I needed to create an environment where breaking the rules was allowed. One where I could be wearing curlers as my brand on my LinkedIn profile. Where I controlled my own path.

Going from employee, to consultant, to true business owner of a presentation and consulting company has not been an overnight process. Fear kept me back from going as fast as I could have, and fear continues to cause me to doubt. But I am true to myself now. If you are looking for a stoic speaker, I am not the fit. But if you are looking for someone who uses humor as a tool to engage, connect, and educate, then I'm your gal. My authenticity and personality are right out there on my Twitter feed, my website, and everywhere else. Like or hate it. But I own it.

The ONLY thing that has held me back is my own belief in myself. Sure, at times I would have said money, but that is only because I did not believe that I could make it work. At other times, I would have said new business, but that is only because I was afraid to apply for it.

When momentum is on your side, maximize it! We all go through peaks and valleys. What we do in the peaks will keep the valleys from being deserts. I am still afraid that you might judge me for using curlers in my profile pictures. I still worry about whether a story is "funny" or not. But I don't doubt that you'll remember me.

Your little childhood dream is waiting on the other side of that villain with the mustache. In fact, it might even be Fear shouting at you to "pay the rent!" But remember this: You are not the damsel. You are the hero. I can already hear Fear say, "Curses…foiled again!"

Rebecca is a Speaker, Author and Business Consultant with the message of putting fun back in business.

Take Action. Grow Big!

» The Results Map starts with three simple yet powerful fundamentals: perspective, strategy and results. These fundamentals will guide you as you approach each exercise and build your Map to success.

» Follow the proven process. Read every chapter and do not skip activities.

Notes

_____

_____

_____

_____

_____

Chapter 2
Fear of the Horizon

"Fear had nothing left to take and suddenly, fear moved on."
-Krissy Ferro

The Results Map Fundamental: Perspective

I need a coat because it's getting a little chilly. Fear strikes again and most women I know have some serious frostbite. I did a survey through social media around what women in biz struggle with the most. The rankings were: having enough capital, having the knowledge needed to build a biz, and drum roll please, number 1 was fear. This is not a shock, as we women tend to live in it, and for no apparent good reason.

Call me crazy, but I have a love of fear. I embrace it with open arms. I experience it every day and I am grateful that I do. It may sound odd to be excited about what we would assume is a negative emotion. I choose my fear to keep me uncomfortable, allowing me to stretch higher, wider, and deeper toward my planned accomplishments. This can mean breaking out of your comfort zone and going after what you really want...or not.

So what if you stumble? So what if you fall? So what if you get hurt? Really ladies, so what? My intention is not to sound heartless. My objective is to take a blow dryer to that frost bite and get you moving. Listen gals, I have stumbled, I have fallen and yes I have gotten hurt. I stumbled by taking risks. I took a few falls financially. I got hurt in relationships. Interestingly enough, I'm still here, I'm alive and well, and fired up to share my experiences with you. Guess what? From those experiences emerged a new life for my biz and a new perspective for my growth.

In biz, you have to be okay with falling and failing

In The Results Map program, you will learn where you can find your safety net, should you need it. Just like in everything I teach around perspective; it starts with you. Like I said in Chapter One, it's time to get uncomfortable! In this chapter you will learn how to squash your fears by allowing tough choices to be easier. You'll stop living in guilt and playing a victim, and learn how to put fear to work in the right way. I have seen brilliant business owners fail because of this very emotion. Break through the fear and allow your biz the growth it deserves.

Biz and life come with making choices and changes. One choice can change the entire outcome of your biz and your life. Lisa Nichols says it best, "I'm not extraordinary. I'm simply an ordinary woman who chooses every day to make extraordinary decisions." Being clear on why and how you make choices is important in developing your Map.

People often forget that they have the power to make choices, to own them, and to take action on them. The average person makes up to 35,000 choices per day. That probably seems like a lot of choices, but think about the process of going out for dinner. First, you decide where to go and what time, then table or booth, what to drink, whether or not to get an appetizer, then decide on a dinner choice, soup or salad, finish your plate or get a to-go box. That's eight decisions, just for dinner. And in reality, you probably make more choices than that when you go out to eat. We make choices by the minute, all day, every day.

So what happens when you come to a choice that isn't as easy as picking a soup or a salad? Let me give you another example. Have you ever been stuck considering if you should pitch a deal to a prospective client? Are you qualified? Do you have the staff in place to manage the deal if you get it? How should you cost it out? Will your decisions inhibit growth within other accounts? The list goes on and on. Making choices and changes can be challenging when it is not clear where you are heading or where you want to land. Making choices is easier when you are clear on what you want and understand the steps you need to take to get there. We will take a deep dive in future chapters to become crystal clear on what you want.

An average of twenty seven choices per day take up to nine minutes to make. That's four hours of contemplation time each day. That is a lot of brainpower clouding up clarity and leaving you frustrated about your next steps. Have you ever come home to your family at the end of the day only to be asked, "What do you want for dinner?" You then dive into a deep spiral and proclaim you cannot make one more single decision! This should be a clear sign that you are struggling to make choices. But you're not alone. Everybody gets tired of making choices. They can be exhausting. This does not mean that clarifying your Results Map will spare you difficult choices. Instead, you will be more confident, clear and secure in making them.

For example, I was offered a long term, high-level consulting contract with a company. It would be more money than I had made in my previous career, and a great opportunity to exercise everything I had done in my past. I turned it down in about two minutes flat. Was I crazy? No. The quick and easy route would have been to take the immediate offering; the easy road. After hearing the offer, I was able to turn it down because it was not a part of my Map and planned accomplishments. Financially it was the immediate win, but it would take me off track and away from what I wanted to accomplish long term. I wanted to reach broad audiences, and help as many women as possible grow and prosper. I could not accomplish that if I dedicated all of my time to one company. This is a prime example of being crystal clear in knowing what you want in order to make the right choices. Don't get me wrong, immediate wins can bring short term and long term gain, but these gains should always be considered alongside your Map.

The Question you need to ask yourself is, "Does it fall in line with my planned accomplishments?"

There are several areas where decision-making becomes difficult. First, let's touch on guilt and playing the victim card.

First is guilt. Have you ever been focused on eating healthy? On day two, you end up breaking down and eating that cupcake for dessert or ordering a martini with dinner? You chose to deviate from your plan. With every drink or bite you feel like you've failed. You can't even enjoy the treat in front of you. This can be incredibly damaging. When you are making strong, clear choices, it can alleviate these negative emotions and behaviors.

When you make a choice, live in it, relish in it, and own it!

If you are going to veer from your plan, own the decision. Enjoy the drink or the cupcake and reset your mind. Don't focus on the failure. Instead focus on how to get back on course the next day. Ladies, we self-sabotage and beat ourselves up way too often. Whenever you tell yourself, "I can't," "I failed," I will never," etc., your brain will remember and believe it. Be kind to yourself and instead of all that negative talk, say, "I can, I will and I won."

You will not believe how empowered you will feel by owning your choices.

One thing to caution you on: just because you are crystal clear on making and owning your choices, doesn't mean you can't consider how they will affect other people. Your journey will affect many, so always make your choices wisely and responsibly.

Next, the victim card. Do you understand that you have the right to make choices and have the ability to make changes? I don't intend to sound condescending, but I want to bring the awareness that yes, you do! The sense of "victimization" sits deep inside and can poison our sense of accomplishments and disempower us from making the correct choices in life and in the workplace.

Some people wallow in the sense of victimization and it is almost impossible to move forward when this happens. I tend to drive my family crazy with the "no victim zone" declared in my home. If someone starts wallowing, I simply proclaim, "choices". They'll reel it in, discovering a solution to the issue, most often with a choice that needs to be made. Ironically, my family will announce it back to me too and I love it! I'm always up for a nice dose of perspective!

Let me give you an example. You are running late because of traffic. You miss your appointment and you lose the deal. You curse the traffic, but really, you didn't allow for traffic time. Being a victim is really about a lack of accountability. Everything is everyone else's fault, when really it is *us* making the wrong choices. That morning, hitting the snooze button five times instead of getting up, you slept in and ran late. The choice to sleep in versus getting on the road at the right time was what lost you the deal.

So again, own your choices!

If you don't, they will add weight to your life, decrease your effectiveness, hold you back from what you want and allow fear to emerge. Life is too short to work hard and end up empty handed in the end.

Own your stuff.

The toughest choices to make are emotional choices: family, friends, finance, and future. Why do people find it difficult to make choices around these four areas? The reasons for these difficulties are varied, but mostly involve fear, stress, personal history, and discomfort with the unknown. Many people don't want to deal with certain things, so they don't. The need to make choices and take action will sit in your subconscious until you are forced to make decisions quickly and with apprehension. When your Map is clear, even these tougher, emotion-driven choices come easier. This doesn't mean that you do not consider other people's feelings or potential outcomes. What it does is help you approach these tougher areas with the ability to make wiser, more confident decisions and to take action from them.

So, how do you take normally tough choices and make them easier? Working with family, friends, finance and future can be as difficult as you choose to make it. Three words can change all of this: perspective, strategy and results!

Consider these three steps when making a difficult choice in any situation:

1. Perspective: Assess the situation with black and white facts. Sometimes charting it on a piece of paper helps. And remember to take your feelings and emotions out of it. What is the current situation and what needs to be done?

2. Strategy: Now that you understand the full scope of the situation, look at how it can be handled. What is your role in this? What are the roles that others play in this situation? Maybe look at different approaches with other possible outcomes. Again, stick to the facts, drop the emotion and discard anything with accusations.

3. Results: Now you know what needs to be done and how you will handle it. The next step is how will you take action? Do you need support from other people or do you need to research additional information? Do you need to bring notes to the meeting or call to keep you on track? Take a deep breathe and keep calm. Stick to the facts and you will not only get through it, but you will be confident in your choices and in control of the meeting.

Removing the emotion from any situation and staying mindful of the facts in front of you will enable effective choices to be made

Sometimes we need to make tough choices and do the hard work to change. Let's put fear to work in the right way. Often times we are wound up and stressed out, frozen in fear and not quite sure what the heart of the matter even is. Don't give fear the power. Will you squash fear or let it fuel you?

Today's progress is determined by yesterday's choices.

Certain seasons and tough days can throw you for a loop and often times it's hard to snap out of it. Fear is an emotion and a state of mind. It can be scary to embrace the unknown or a new idea that you are testing. There is a solution 99.99% of the time.

Exercise

Let's explore how to conquer fear and use it to your advantage. Fill in the blanks below in each step.

**Note, for all printable exercises within The Results Map book, go to KimberlyAlexanderInc.com

STEP 1: IDENTIFY

Identify what is holding you back. Listed below are a few thoughts-starters:

New venture, new city, losing focus, losing money, perception from others, unknown, success, nay-sayers, can't think past yourself, belief in yourself

_____

_____

_____

_____

_____

STEP 2: REASON

Why is your fear freezing you? Listed below are some examples:

Could lose business, could lose respect, could lose the house, people may not take me seriously

_____

_____

_____

_____

_____

STEP 3: SOLUTION

What are some activities you can do to work past it? Listed below are some thought-starters:

Talk it through with a coach or friend, research, investigate, plan and strategize

_____

_____

_____

_____

_____

STEP 4: RESULTS

What will change in result of overcoming your fear?

Increase in biz, develop a new skill, meet new people

_____

_____

_____

_____

_____

I know this exercise was not easy. It is never a simple exercise in facing your fears and emotions. When you feel you are freezing up, come back to this exercise again and again. Own your fears and let them drive you to do what you were meant to do.

The smallest of tweaks to your biz will allow you to soar higher than you could imagine. One choice could change the entire outcome of your biz and life. It all starts with you and identifying possibilities. Keep reading and you will find them.

Krissy Ferro
FerroCosmetics.com

I have been through a lot of colorful ups and downs, more than most my age. There has been nothing that has tested me more, challenged me more, taken more, and strained relationships more than the events of life and occurrences of building my company. I have been denied promises, failed, and my faith has been tested. I could probably write one full novel for each year's events, tragedies and triumphs alone. I handled challenges I never knew I had the strength to endure. Of all of them, the only one that could have slayed it all, was the one I could control and tame throughout the entire journey. Of all of the wins and misses, the biggest challenge of my life has been the battle against fear.

In late 2006, I could feel the inner brewing of something huge. I spoke with my husband, about an idea I had to launch a new business and I had a feeling this could be a major opportunity. My husband was a tortured, beautiful soul. He was constantly battling the good and the evil. He believed in me and loved me, yet was extremely torn on how to handle my will when I got an idea and saw it through. He was especially threatened if I had ideas of making us financially independent, which to him, meant that I would leave. He had an utter fear of being alone.

In 2007, I still felt so strongly about the calling of my ideas for a new company that I closed my eyes and jumped in. My husband was not ready for that kind of jump. We separated, intending to eventually work our way back to each other. The toxic energy was too much for too long, and I had two young boys that I didn't want influenced by such a challenging environment.

That summer, Ferro Cosmetics was born. My studio turned into a lab, and that was the first summer my family wasn't outside in our pool. My mom was with me in my "lab" and the boys mixed up their fun creations with me all summer. We didn't have a tan and we barely saw the pool. Mom would say, "We have to wait until next year to float, never again will we miss family time at the pool" I enthusiastically agreed, "Never is Right!"

My father believed in me, and in my mission, enough to partner with me and help fund the launch of Ferro Cosmetics in 2007. My cousins, aunts, everyone who was there in the beginning, were all in. It is not easy launching a cosmetics company and the pressure and stress to deliver was growing by the day. There was fierce energy I started calling "Ferro Fever".

We launched online in October 2007, with barely any online sales to show for it. This was interesting, since it is an "e-commerce only" business. Yet by the fifth month, I met my good friend Carrie Stevens via email. With her influence, three days later I was on a plane doing a cosmetics event, and sleeping at her house. We never met before. She felt good about it, so did I, and bam, I was doing color for 13 playmates in Carries online magazine. It was my first time near celebrities, in Beverly Hills, and seeing my makeup in action.

Dreams come true.

As the business continued to grow, I was asked to be on a TV show launch that would warp speed my business forward. I couldn't believe it, Ferro Cosmetics was going national and on TV! Sadly, I was taken advantage of by this opportunity. It was all a scam, resulting in financial ruin for my family. We were taken for everything we had. I lost it all and while this was happening, my husband was not getting better. His depression was getting the best of him. Although we were separated, I of course wished for his well-being.

It started spiraling out of control. I realized there were many areas of my business I that had not protected, researched, or secured. I had investors on my back, issues with our warehouse, and my family to tend to. I craved normalcy for my boys, all while fear continued to fester, brew, and grow deep inside of me as I pressed on, never letting the dream die.

I was left feeling depleted, battered, and everyone else was so angry with me. There was a wicked stench in the air, and I was happy to be leaving for my photo shoot. Just into my shoot, my staff crumbled and a quick fix to increase sales took the company down even further.

I wasn't giving up. I had just recently moved into a new home, my boys were in a great school, the sun was shining, and I was ready and open for possibilities. Then the world flipped and tilted and screeched into a nightmare. My husband, who I just talked to for three hours the previous night, who seemed to have gotten rid of his demons and was ready to come home, left this world. Left his boys. Left me to raise them…alone. After that, I went completely numb.

I started grieving my husband four years later, although could only handle anger at first. 2014 is when the forgiveness came, and the love, and everything my numb state had me protected from. I was surprised to find the grief was so beautiful even when it was painful. I never expected to feel everything, even joy.

If I could go back, with the knowledge I have gained, I would do some things differently. I would have and will be open to learning every day. I would have shared my loving intentions for everyone, and I would have stated what it's going to take to get it as a team. I would have pushed back the fear and allowed myself to expect more from vendors, consultants and employees. I would have asked for help sooner, and not felt weak because of it. I would have held my ground because I would have known I could stand on it. I would not fear being left alone or having to handle everything on my own. And as I write and still have much left to reclaim, I would still lose it all again, if that's what it took to make my spirit free of fear.

My "crazy" is my calling, my genius, and my failures are my battle stars, not scars. I let fear live and eat away at everything until it ate everything completely. When it was gone, fear had nothing left to take and suddenly, fear moved on.

Krissy is the Founder and CEO of Ferro Cosmetics, an on-line Cosmetics company

Take Action. Grow Big!

» Making the choice to change is critical in either moving forward toward your planned accomplishments or holding yourself back.
» Keep emotion out of making choices
» You can strategically make choices and take action to change through the system of perspective, strategy and results
» No victims or guilt allowed!
» Understanding your fears and how they impact your choices in your biz and your life are a critical step in taking the right actions.

Notes

_____

_____

_____

_____

_____

CHAPTER 3

HEAVY WEIGHT

---

*"What I know now is we all have that choice
and the power within to make it.*
-Nicole Montez

The Results Map Fundamental: Perspective

You are on your way. You are making the trek up the next path, headed for the summit, and for some reason you cannot take one step further. You're exhausted, beaten down and feel like there is a force weighting you to the ground. You stop to take a rest. It must be the hard work and tireless hours you have put in to get to this point, to reach the summit, the sunshine, and the destination. You pause for a moment and reach for your water, but instead find rocks. Tons of rocks, big and small, rough and smooth; it looks to be from different mountainsides. That's it, that's the issue. The rocks were holding you back and wearing you down. Rocks that you have collected along the way, adding them to your pack over years of time. You realize there is no water needed. You ditch the rocks, and with a new heightened level of determination and lighter pack, you continue up the path, aiming for the summit.

We women just don't know what to do with the past. We often refer to our past as baggage or heavy weight. Now, whether you have great or challenging things in your past, we often default to heavy weight as the baggage that sticks with you and carries you to the next phase of your biz and life. Believe it or not, positive, fantastic things are baggage too. These are referred to as successes, wins, and lessons. It's all baggage; we just perceive every piece of our lives differently. The good baggage may be regarded as an expensive bag, while the challenging baggage would be considered an old throw away one. What you will learn in this chapter is that every piece of baggage in your life matters and is necessary for the journey of who you are intended to become. When leveraged correctly, it will elevate you while warp-speeding your biz and life forward.

Are you the woman who carries her rocks to endless mountaintops, if she can even reach it at all? Or do you dump the rocks and move forward more freely and with a greater stride? The answer should be no to both. People make choices daily if not hourly based on past experiences. Is this sub-conscience behavior helping you or hurting you?

Learn from your past to thrive in your future.

This really is true. Are there actions you should stop taking or continue doing to grow your biz and your personal development? In this Chapter you will learn how to answer these questions.

The past and baggage tend to be referred to in a negative connotation. We all have something unfavorable from our past that holds us back. Yes, bad things happen, but great and incredible things happen to us too. Not to sound condescending, but this is something we refer to as life. Life happens whether by plan, no plan, smart decisions, or tough decisions. We need a balance of both to keep the expectation and awareness of what happiness, fear, joy, disappointment, and success means to us, as well as how we keep it in check. In the essence of figuring this whole life-thing out, we need to embrace that yes, challenging experiences happen by the choices we make, the situations we put ourselves in, the company we keep, the money we spend, the food we eat, and the risks we take.

Let me give you an idea of what I'm talking about. In 2008 and 2009 our national economy was in a downfall at warp speed. Our family, friends, and colleagues were losing businesses, houses, jobs, retirement, marriages, security and happiness. Everywhere you turned, businesses were influenced by a ripple effect of loss. My husband owns two pizza joints that are more upscale than the average five-dollar delivery deal. Customers stopped visiting his well-established restaurants because a fourteen dollar pizza was well out of their budget. Every possible industry imaginable was affected and some still are. It was a scary time of uncertainty and utter fear.

I was working in the corporate arena at the time in the luxury goods business. I was launching a new brand into the market place, making incredible contacts and developing the business above expectations. Business and life were good and then, like the flip of a switch, the lights went out.

It seems as if it were overnight, the business came to a screeching halt. Clients disappeared, vendors couldn't deliver, and our warehouse inventory started collecting dust. Just like the fourteen dollar pizza, companies couldn't sell high-end luxury items. I saw the writing on the wall, and started updating my resume. The President of the company visited me one Friday afternoon to sadly ask me to clear my desk. My position was being diminished.

Like autopilot, I reached out to contacts, relationships, and friends. Within two weeks I had three job offers on the table, and within three weeks, those three offers went on hold. For the first time in my career and life I had a fear of finding a job and wondering where money would come from. My next step was to tackle job boards, headhunters, and looking for part-time work.

First day into unemployment I got a job waiting tables. I served burgers to enthusiastic families, usually with a few kids in tow, balloons tied to their wrists and endless baskets of fries at their table. The staff consisted of mostly laid off executives like me, all doing the same thing, trying to keep the lights on and food on the table for their families. I was positive and optimistic for the first six months, vowing to never settle for less and that the right opportunity was waiting for me. At month seven, absolute fear set in. Our savings were spent, revenue from our restaurants was lean, and I was making very little on tips. The reality of losing everything set in and I froze. I was reduced to tears every time I needed to put gas in my car. I went to the grocery store with a calculator so I knew I would stay within our tight budget. I felt completely helpless all the while working tirelessly to solve the issue.

A few months later I was hired and within a year we were in a good, solid positon again. We didn't lose anything like our house, cars, or self-respect. I learned many lessons, and yet adopted one big thing…heavy weight and lots of baggage. I carried with me that old baggage that no one wants, the fearful, reactionary, helpless baggage. I didn't realize I carried this with me until month ten in the first year of my business. I had adopted a new-found syndrome that I now call Resume Syndrome. A syndrome that entrepreneurs adopt when building a brand and a biz gets incredibly hard, almost unreachable to the dream. When money runs out, resources grow scarce, clients disappear or a network dries up. Worse than ever, is when the fear overcomes the belief.

I leaped out of the gates when I launched my brand with clients, speaking in engagements and a lot of Public Relations. I launched my first book that went bestseller and was elated beyond words. Then that switch turned off again. I shared with my mentors over and over again that I might have to go back to work. I had to start planning how I could build my brand and business while working an executive job. What I quickly realized is that I was holding onto the bad baggage, those heavy rocks were in my pack. Instead of learning from it and gaining experience from it, it fueled me to give up and to live in financial fear. My husband came to me one day and said, "You're either all in, or get out". That was a massive wakeup call for me, big time. This fear from 2008 and 2009 of going back to reaction mode had a dramatic, negative impact on me. I believed what I was meant to do, and in myself, but Resume Syndrome was holding me back from doing great things for a lot of people. So I changed my perspective and the rest is history. In fact, a month later my business skyrocketed yet again. Perspective wins the race.

Perspective is about getting to the heart of the matter. How can you plan when you don't know what you stand for? What are you really willing to do to get it? Like "All in or get out", does your belief in all that you do carry you past Resume Syndrome or any other syndrome you may experience? Some people freeze or fall into severe depression. I've seen it all. Perspective fuels you to learn from the hits and misses in your biz and life, just like we discussed in Chapter two about fear. Most often the misses built my biz quicker and stronger; it's all a matter in how you look at it.

Taking on a different perspective from carrying baggage versus leveraging baggage starts with awareness. Being aware of your thoughts and actions, as well as the good and challenging baggage. How will you leverage these experiences and lessons to your benefit? Back to Resume

Syndrome. When times get tough and hard, don't jump into reaction mode or go for the quick fix. Instead, stop, take a breath and walk through opportunities in front of you to look for the long-term solutions. Often times we don't realize the doors right in front of us that we can open immediately. Awareness of your behaviors in reaction, fear, or freezing mode will put up walls and take you down a path you don't want to go down. There are no quick fixes. Do the hard work and stay on course.

Now let's chat about learning. I am so passionate about learning! What have you learned? Whether you experienced a win or lose, success or failure, victory or defeat, what is the lesson? When I am hosting a call, training, a workshop, or a meeting I will always recap and ask myself, "What went well and what could be improved?" It takes courage to receive feedback from others or yourself. We always want to think that we nailed it and need no improvement. Think about this, if you always showed up 100% on top of your game, would you ever learn, grow, and improve the person you are? Don't you always strive to become an even better version of who you are today? If your answer is yes, then understand that it will take trying new things, trusting in others, seeking out knowledge, and working on your own personal development. I always say, "I can't wait to see where I am at this time next year". Every year I take inventory of what I learned and how much further I grew in my own development. It's exciting and is what gets me out of bed in the morning. I have made fantastic decisions and really bad ones too. It's okay; both of those lead me to the here and now, better than I was this time last year. Think about it, what has lead you here and what is taking you to the next level of success, whether good or challenging from your past? Whether you have good or bad baggage, always allow the lessons for growth.

Exercise

Identify how to leverage your baggage. Take your time with this exercise. This is a tool to grow your future.

**Note, for all printable exercises within The Results Map book, go to KimberlyAlexanderInc.com

1. IDENTIFY A BIG CHALLENGE YOU ARE FACING IN YOUR BIZ OR LIFE

Example: Won't invest into your biz, won't take a risk, will not hire an expert, will not get feedback from peers or mentor

_____

_____

_____

_____

_____

2. IDENTIFY WHY IT IS A CHALLENGE (NORMALLY THIS IS AN EMOTION)

Example: Fear, rejection, the unknown)

_____

_____

_____

_____

_____

3. HOW IS THIS IMPACTING YOUR BIZ OR LIFE?

Example: Decrease in biz, hard to plan, can't sleep, feel like a failure, loss of revenue

_____

_____

_____

_____

_____

4. WHAT WILL YOU DO TO OVERCOME THIS CHALLENGE TO REALIZE YOUR LESSONS LEARNED?

Example: Mentorship, journaling, research

_____

_____

_____

_____

_____

5. WHEN WILL YOU TAKE ACTION?

Example: Today, tomorrow, next week…no later!

_____

_____

_____

_____

_____

Ladies, move forward the way you were intended. Leverage your baggage to work with you and for you, not against you. Allow your lessons to fuel your calling and purpose. Understanding why you make certain decisions in order to grow your business will help break down the walls and enable you to grow further than you have ever imagined. Every piece of baggage or heavy weight in your life is good. When it is leveraged correctly it will elevate and warp speed your business and life. Really, having baggage brings lessons, learning, challenges and experiences. They create the person we have become or strive to be. So I say again, the past is tricky, but when you leverage your heavy weight and learn from your past you will thrive in your future.

Your past doesn't define you. It gives you roots to grow to greatness.

Nicole Montez
NicoleKMontez.com

I was the girl that always knew I would be a CEO. I was going to climb the corporate ladder, and I had a plan. All the way back to when I was the little girl proudly pushing my books in my baby stroller while my friends were happily pushing their baby dolls. I strived through school and business college, and found a career I which soon thrived in. I got engaged and kept my plan to reach my business goals, and knew one day *maybe* we would raise a family. It wasn't long before my husband and I shockingly learned that we were having a baby. This was not part of my plan; I was just 24 and certainly hadn't even begun to reach my career goals. Remember, I pushed books in my stroller, not babies. Now here I was, a soon-to-be mom. Never did it occur to me our baby wouldn't be healthy. I nonchalantly nodded in agreement to the doctor, having all the pregnancy tests done. Of course nothing would be wrong with my baby. This wasn't even part of my plan, I was destined to climb the corporate ladder, and I still intended to do so. As I settled into expecting a baby, and even became excited with such an easy pregnancy, I continued to work and plan my future. Of course the plan was to take the normal, expected maternity leave, and then find a nurturing, equipped nanny to take care of our baby throughout the day. A total win-win! We had a plan!

At 37 weeks I delivered the most beautiful blue eyed and red haired baby girl we named Alexandra. We proudly took her home a bright sunny spring day in May 2001. I couldn't believe it. I was now a mom, and I was committed to my new calling. Everything was as it should have been until that afternoon when she was just 2 weeks old. That day had changed everything, for me, for her. For all of us. The doctor called to inform us Alex had tested positive for a genetic disease called Cystic Fibrosis. A disease? My daughter? It couldn't be. Two days later I found myself at Denver Children's Hospital with bands of gauze wrapped around her wrists as doctors tested her sweat for the amount of salt that excretes from her body, a true measurement for CF. The nurses tried to comfort me, assuring me of all the false positive results that often happen. They felt sorry for me being a young, scared mom when everything is usually all okay when the tests come out negative. Later that week my husband and I found ourselves in a stale, cold, white hospital room where four people entered the room. The head Cystic Fibrosis doctor, the head nurse, a social worker, and a nutritionist to inform us that Alex did indeed have a fatal, genetic disease called Cystic Fibrosis. She will always carry more mucus in her lungs and will never digest fat. She would one day need a lung transplant and always struggle to maintaining weight, needing enzymes to digest her food. I held on to Alex who was only about 1 ½ half feet long still in the curled fetal position lying on my chest. A lifetime with a disease? Possibly a *short* lifetime? They told us the average age for someone born with CF today was 37 years old. 50% survive childhood, which was supposed to be an improvement when, only a few years ago, most would have only lived to be school aged. The cost of her care would be millions of dollars over a lifetime. How was I supposed to feel? How could this be part of the plan? How would I take care of her? Would she die before me? I couldn't even hear anything else they told me. I was too worried about how I would raise her. How would we afford her? How would I find the strength to be the mom she needed. How is this happening to me? No more books in the baby stroller. Not even a baby, but a baby with a fatal disease. My Alex. My life. Not my plan.

I had many breakdowns over the weeks that followed; many tears, thoughts, conversations. I learned everything I could about Cystic Fibrosis. I decided to be a stay-at-home-mom. I needed to be with her every moment I could. It was in one of the moments where I knew I had to make a difference. I had to take control and make sure her diagnosis wasn't her destiny. Although my plan was to be a corporate CEO, perhaps now I would have to become the CEO of my own life, and of her life. I made a choice to find something where I could earn an income at home.

It's not a surprise I would align with a wellness business. Here I saw the potential and the dream of replacing my income; the income I gave up to raise Alex.

It all started with a choice. No one called me with an option, or a job, or handed us money. I had to pick myself off my soaked tear-filled bed and become non-negotiable about my success, and most of all, her life and destiny. What I know now is we all have that choice and the power within to make it.

I was terrified. I was venturing into new territory without mentors to help me find the way. I never did sales or marketing, and no one was going to make me do it. It was entirely up to me. My biggest struggle was balancing my life as the mom of a daughter with special needs, and the growing pains of becoming an entrepreneur. It's lonely when you work from home and there isn't a friend to grab a coffee with, or an office full of chatter.

There were moments I doubted myself, many moments where I felt like I was banging my head against the wall, but I couldn't stop. This was for Alex. No obstacle was too great. After all how could I expect her to overcome a lifetime of her obstacles, if I couldn't overcome mine?

Over the course of daily intentional activity into my new business I grew to replace my income in just over a year. The following year replaced and more than tripled my husband's income. He retired from his career to be home and with Alex.

The greatest lessons I've learned in my entrepreneur journey is to never stop growing. Take even just 15 minutes a day to read powerful books and messages from those farther along in their journey, and continue to raise your level of leadership. Remember to ask for help when you need it. I think this is the number one issue we have as female entrepreneurs - we feel we can do it all.

Know you are good enough. Good enough for your goals, your dreams, your family, your children, and your business. You deserve it and you are called to do it. You are called to give it all you have.

I'm so grateful for Alex. Today she is a thriving 14 year old with a dream of becoming a professional dancer. She dances more than 30 hours a week and still maintains above average lung function, beating so many odds. I know without a doubt the power we have when we make a choice. I can't say I would change her diagnosis. I would, without a doubt, take away every single second of her suffering. However, without her Cystic Fibrosis we wouldn't truly know how blessed we are, what we are capable of, and what we are called to do.

Nicole is an Entrepreneur, Speaker, and Non-Negotiable Success Leader

Take Action. Grow Big!

» Every piece of baggage in your life matters and is necessary for the journey of who you are meant to become.
» When leveraged correctly, your heavy weight will elevate you, while warp speeding your biz and life forward
» Be aware of your thoughts and actions and both your good and challenging baggage.
» Whether you experienced a win or lose, success or failure, victory or defeat, what are the lessons? Learn from them to move you forward.

Notes

_____

_____

_____

_____

_____

CHAPTER 4
GET CLEAR

"I took my pain and I turned it into my purpose and passion."
-Pamela Zimmer

The Results Map Fundamental: Perspective

It's 3:00am and there it is again; awake. It's now several nights in a row and at 3:00am your brain ignites, waking you up and making you think. As you shuffle to the coffee maker, your body is heavy, but your mind is alive and thriving. There are always so many thoughts jumping in and out of your consciousness. You finally wave the white flag, get out your computer, journal, or notepad and start writing. You write and write and write and write. Every so often there are tears streaming down your face and perhaps a smile too. Ideas that seem unreachable pour from your mind, but you stay the course and keep writing. The words start to scare you and seem like they might be a little over the top, but you press on. After minutes, even hours, and possibly a coffee pot later, you look up.

There before you lies your purpose.

Do you really know what purpose is? Your purpose won't let you give up and doesn't care what other people think. It is calling you to do great things. As Oprah so wisely quotes, *"Follow your passion. It will lead you to your purpose."* Purpose will lead you down the right path to do what you were meant to do.

I open up this chapter with happy tears, tears of joy and bliss and excitement and wonder and amazement. The reason for this wave of sweet emotion is the thought of all women reading this book to find their purpose.

In this chapter, you will identify your purpose and the next steps to take in your journey. How do you embrace it and what do you do with it. You may find it and think, well, what now? You may already know what your purpose is, but it will come even clearer when you know how to best serve with it. Ladies, your perspective on your biz and life is about to heighten, elevate, and ignite. 3:00am doesn't happen by chance. It is something bigger than you.

Purpose is so important in your biz and in your life. It really is the starting point in everything that you do in order to make the right decisions and to move down the right path every single day. Many women aren't quite sure what their purpose is. Some women call it your purpose, and others, your calling, even a higher power. Whatever it may be, this is the type of work that is fun and exciting for you. It doesn't feel taxing and it doesn't feel like work. It feels like something that just energizes you and fills you up with the thrill to jump into each day.

Let's get clear and start identifying your purpose. Here are a few thought starters:

What do you love to do?

Do you find that you are guiding or coaching people to things that currently are not in your field or practice?

Is there something in the back of your mind that you dream of and can't stop thinking about?

Did you live through an experience that has forever changed and stirred you to the core?

Is there a message deep inside of you that should make its mark in the world?

This very thing happened to me. I had a biz that I loved, but found that I was doing a lot of free side-work in the areas that I was so much more passionate about. A few people reached out to me and said, "What are you doing? You really aren't working your life's calling." It woke me up! I wasn't aware of my actions or how I really wanted to be in a totally different line of work. I listened and evolved into the brand that I am today. My destiny is to live my best life as I teach others to do the same.

Is your destiny calling?

Exercise

Identify your purpose.

*Note, for all printable exercises within The Results Map book, go to KimberlyAlexanderInc.com

1. WHAT DO YOU LOVE TO DO?

Stop. Ponder. Brainstorm...

(Some of my best ideas came from being lost in thought.)

_____

_____

_____

_____

_____

Marie Forleo nails it, "If it's not a hell yes, it's a no." Be aware of the actions that you're taking every day. Take note of the work that you get really excited about.

2. WHAT ACTIONS ARE YOU TAKING OUTSIDE OF YOUR CURRENT ROLE?

Stop. Ponder. Brainstorm...

_____

_____

_____

_____

_____

As you peruse through the internet, social media or even networking opportunities, what articles are you reading and groups are you joining? What captures your attention?

3. WHO DO YOU LOVE TO SERVE?

Stop. Ponder. Brainstorm…

_____

_____

_____

_____

_____

This is huge in determining what you want to do and who you want to be. You may know your targeted audience even before you know how you want to best serve them. Or you may know what you want to do, but not whom it would best benefit. I have seen clients that went from Corporate America to launching their own non-profit business and working with children. Your purpose will not let you give up! Some categories to think of: Age range, male or female, experience or education level.

4. WHAT IS YOUR PURPOSE?

Stop. Ponder. Brainstorm…

_____

_____

_____

_____

_____

It takes courage to identify your purpose and let it out. You may not be ready for it and that is okay. When you follow your purpose, when you follow your passion, decisions come much easier. You'll be able to live that life you want and to drive that biz you want to build.

Okay, ladies, please pay full attention to this next message. It's "line in the sand" time. It's owning who you are meant to be without fail time. It's standing true to you time. There will be times that people will be uncomfortable with your purpose, mission, and vision. They will stand on the sidelines of your path watching, waiting, and listening to see what you are going to do. Often times they are threatened by your ability to not only think big, but to take the action to go big. Sadly, these people love you, but are uncomfortable with your success and your willingness to put yourself out there. Do not take this personally. We call this a thick skin, and focus on how we react to someone else's behavior. I'm not a fan of being reactionary.

I'm a believer in being visionary!

Instead of building up that thick skin, stay mindful of your journey. I'm going to repeat that…stay mindful of YOUR journey! Now this message doesn't mean to not allow coaching and feedback. It's being aware of those nay-sayers that in some sad way, don't want you to succeed. Big-time difference. As a speaker and an author, I'm wide open in the world. It amazes me that people will go out of their way to point out the tiniest of flaws.

Heads up girlfriends, we're not perfect!

Honestly, who wants to be? You will know when it's to help you or hurt you. Let it roll off of your back and keep rolling! I assume most people come from a good place and want to help. Others don't. Either way, it's their stuff. Do not let others trip you up and take you off your course.

Your belief is all that matters.

One more thing to get to the heart of the matter on, and this is a big one for me. Do not fake it till you make it. I have never understood this type of mentality and never will. Think about what this statement is saying; that you are misrepresenting yourself until you really know what you're doing. I am truly laughing out loud at this moment, just thinking about it. You have one reputation. Make it honest, and let it be built from your hard work, passion, and real knowledge. Be authentic.

So, how do you show up as your authentic, wonderful self? Is it with the existing skills that you possess and the value that you bring to the table? Focus on who you are now. Don't fake it until you make anything. Work to improve your skill, your talent, and your knowledge and only then you can evolve into bigger things down the road. But until then, show up as fabulous you and what you offer today. Tomorrow will come, I promise. If you want to be bigger and better, seek out the people that will help get you there. Chapter Five will help you in identifying how to accomplish that. Until then, own, love and appreciate authentic you.

So what do you need to learn in order to grow? This is important in your journey to identify your purpose. For a dramatic example, if you are working as an Account Executive and have decided you want to become a heart surgeon, you will need to learn a few new things before you see the operating room. The same goes for your biz, but hopefully much less dramatic. To transform into something bigger than yourself, it takes learning, and lessons, and ups, and downs. I'm going to give you some thought starters on what you need to do to grow and move the needle on your biz. You may have all the right plans in place; you're in front of the right people, you're going to all the right types of events, but for some reason it's just not happening.

1. MENTORS

If you find that you're struggling in many areas, mentors can guide you to see things within your biz and yourself that you may not see. Mentors and Coaches can help you identify exactly what it is that you need and in the right time. Everyone needs a biz mentor. I have a biz mentor and even my mentors have mentors. This could be the step you need. Often times you can grow out of mentors and coaches too. Be mindful of this. You will need different mentors, and different types of knowledge and learning throughout your journey.

2. CERTIFICATIONS

Based on your line of work, you may need a certification, program, or added software skill. Have companies or individuals chosen you over someone else because of your credibility? Are you having a hard time selling, planning, or whatever it may be because your knowledge is lacking? For example, it may be an industry skill like IT, social media, PR, or a program. Growing your knowledge within your industry and the needs of your biz will help move it forward quickly.

So ladies, what is it that you need to learn?

_____

_____

_____

_____

Once you identify what it is that you need to learn, consider these four approaches:

Will you apply the learning to your biz on your own?

Will you outsource it with a consultant?

Will you hire an employee to do it?

Will you apply all the above?

You may just need to have an understanding of what it is you need to accomplish and how. It may be the smartest use of your time to hire a consultant to do the work. I have a strong understanding in social media. However, I use marketing experts to support me with those efforts. Be smart with your time and where you can best serve. It's really important to understand where you fall into play on knowledge and skill in order to get the work done to move your biz forward.

So we discussed a lot of intensive thoughts in this chapter: determining your purpose, who you plan to serve, and what steps to take to find your authenticity. If this was your last day on Earth, would you feel that you've lived your life fully? Would you feel that you've fulfilled everything you wanted to accomplish? And lived the life and became the person you had always aspired to be?

Be brave. Be strong. Be courageous!

The purpose of The Results Map is to guide you to live your best life and grow your best biz. It's what wakes you up at 3:00am. Your purpose is your foundation. Set the coffee maker timer to 6:00am instead. Find your purpose and get some rest.

Something bigger than yourself is waiting for you...

Pamela Zimmer
PamelaZimmer.com

Life rarely turns out exactly how you plan it. As children, we often dream about what we want to be when we grow up and who we want to become. We play pretend and imagine our life as this ideal, perfect vision of happiness. Then as we get older, maybe that dream fades into something else, or maybe it gets stronger and stronger until it's a burning fire in your heart that you can't ignore. That's what it was for me.

Ever since I can remember I had always wanted to be a stay-at-home mom. I was highly influenced by my own mom. I admired her, and I wanted to be just like her: loving, caring, and always there for us. I suspect every mom strives to be those three things for her children, and for me it was what I longed for, even before I had met my husband and gotten married.

My dad, a successful international businessman, was also someone I highly admired. I too wanted to have a successful career and make him proud, following in his footsteps, although not entirely on the same career path. I became an Architect and worked in the profession for nearly 13 years, and had my own successful firm for seven and a half of those years. I loved my work. I had a great business partner, but it had started to not be enough.

I met my husband right as I had gone into business for myself. That little voice in my heart kept whispering to me, not letting me forget my dream of being a stay-at-home mom. Just before our second son was born, I left my business and quit my career for motherhood. It was one of the hardest decisions I had ever made, but it was also very freeing.

The transition from career woman to full-time mom was challenging. Not only did I feel like I was losing part of my identity being an architect, but I felt like a first time new mom all over again. I was now the full-time stay-at-home parent, as opposed to when my husband stayed home with our first son, while I went back to work. This is what I had asked for – to be home with our children – but it wasn't what I had expected.

There were challenges, but nothing that I didn't think was abnormal. I was handling new motherhood in stride, and I had my husband's and friends' love and support. But something was wrong. I wasn't happy. Instead, I felt immense guilt, anxiety, and sadness. I cried all the time, and I couldn't sleep despite pure exhaustion and fatigue. I was withdrawn, with a lack of desire to do anything at all. I wasn't taking care of myself and it was everything I could do to muster up the strength and energy to care for our two young boys. I didn't know what was wrong, but I was too afraid to say anything.

Four months after our second son was born I was diagnosed with Postpartum Depression (PPD). Looking back now, I had suffered with PPD for nearly three years, all the way back to when our first son was born, and just never knew.

On a good day, I would get out of bed, maybe change into a clean pair of yoga pants and nursing top, fix myself something to eat, and maybe check in with a friend. Then I would sit on the couch and do my best to nurse Brayden and care for him, but there was always anxiety and self-doubt, and always tears. I cried at everything, and for no good reason. Brayden was my one constant in my life; I knew he needed me to survive. On the bad days it was all I could do to put my focus on him; it took every iota of strength to muster up the energy I needed to care for him. To nurse him, burp him, change him, maybe play with him, and hope to get him to sleep for a nap.

No matter what kind of day it was, I was always scared, guilty, withdrawn, exhausted, ashamed, in physical pain, and always fighting the unwanted thoughts that barged their way into my head, thoughts of leaving or hurting my children. What if I… *took a baseball bat to Zackery? Put Brayden in the dryer? Drove away – with or without them in the car?* These are the thoughts that paralyzed me into silence for fear of being locked up and my children taken away from me. I was terrified of them, and I felt like I was being punished into a fiery hell. For me, these thoughts were the worst part of my PPD, and even knowing now that those thoughts were not my own, I am still sometimes haunted by them. My life was turned upside down. I was a strong, smart, and independent woman. I was not supposed to get PPD. This was not supposed to happen to *me!* This is not how I dreamed my life would be.

It took me almost three more years to completely heal from PPD, but I can honestly say that my pain and suffering opened a whole new opportunity to help other women get over their PPD as well. My experience allowed me to speak up, to have a voice, and to become the voice for other moms who have not yet found their own.

Postpartum Depression is the number one complication associated with pregnancy and childbirth. It is more common than breast cancer, yet it is far less talked about. There is a stigma around PPD that keeps women silent, paralyzed in fear, scared of the judgment. I strive to burst through that stigma.

When I first began my healing, I wrote. I have always loved to write, and that was my outlet. I started with a blog, and eventually began writing a book. It took me two years to write, and it became a number one bestseller on Amazon. It was honestly the most healing thing I ever did. I openly shared my struggle with PPD, my healing process, how it affected those around me, and what I'm doing now.

As moms, and especially entrepreneurial moms, we are always putting ourselves last. Our kids, our husbands, our work, they all come first. It's no wonder we are exhausted, overwhelmed, and burnt out. By teaching and practicing self-care, as well as educating moms about PPD, I am helping them be their best self. Self-care is not selfish; it's necessary. If you don't take care of yourself, you can't possibly serve those around you, those who need you, to your best ability. Moms, and all women, need to learn to put themselves first, without guilt, and by doing so they become better moms.

I started my business as a stay-at-home mom wishing I had someone who knew what I was going through. Amidst all the love and support surrounding me, I never had that one woman who knew exactly what I was experiencing, someone who had been there herself. I wanted to become that woman, so some mom somewhere else wouldn't have to suffer through PPD alone. I took my pain, and I turned it into my purpose and passion.

Pamela is a Speaker, Best-Selling Author and Founder of Love and Mommy Hugs, supporting Moms to break though the burdens of Post Pardom Depression

Take Action. Grow Big!

» Identify what your purpose is.
» Identify the actions are you taking outside of your current role.
» Who would you love to serve?
» Identify additional knowledge needed to build your biz.

Notes

_____

_____

_____

_____

_____

CHAPTER 5
YOUR CREW

"The more you give of yourself, the more you receive of others."
-Kristie Keever

The Results Map Fundamental: Strategy

I received an early Saturday morning text from my dear friend. "You up? Available?" I chuckle at the text; of course I'm up, being the early riser that I am. She responds, "Great, call you in an hour. I just put you on a committee. Need to tell you about it." I'm intrigued. What does she have up her sleeve? So I type back, "Can't wait to hear."

The call came in almost exactly an hour. It's Norah and she is calm, cool and collected, like always. My friend is a larger than life, take on the world type of person, and she does the grandest of things in biz, while always finding pleasure in the simplest things in her life. She is seriously one of my heroes. Greeting me with a,"Hey, Chicka, how are you?" I smile as she has called me this for over 16 years. I give her the cliff notes of how I am; wanting to get to this "committee" she has me so curious about.

"I have breast cancer." Silence. Painful, heart breaking, rock my world silence. I don't know how long it took me to absorb those four words, but she gave me the time to work through the shock. Norah is all business. She begins to tell me next steps of what this all looks like. As I am listening, my body goes numb, my eyes fill with tears, a knot is in my throat and stomach, and my heart begins to ache. I try to be strong for my friend and make sure my voice doesn't crack. Stage one, that's good. My courageous Mom is a survivor of stage one breast cancer. I know it's a tough battle and a long road, even at Stage One. I'm not afraid of cancer beating Norah, but I know what she is walking into it. It's not easy at any stage and it is unknown how she will respond to surgery, chemo, radiation, hair loss, reconstruction, all of it, and I'm not even talking about the emotional pains yet.

Norah talks through all of the medical detail and then says, "I know you call it your crew, but I think I will call mine the Boob Committee. Six women that I need by my side to get through this thing." We burst out laughing. Only Norah, in her style and grace, could assemble her support team, title it, and assign general duties within 24 hours of her diagnosis. My assigned role is to help her keep the biz running in the right perspective in her absence, and to allow her to talk about it. Not many people welcomed biz conversations at first, feeling as if she should be focused on her health. I get it. Her biz is her safe place and she needed it. Check, got it. Kimberly Alexander, Biz Perspective Expert of the Boob Committee, here to serve.

Ladies, you need a crew. Period. You need your inner circle of peeps, both in biz and life. Who has your back no matter what, even when you mess up from time to time?

Who would give anything to see you succeed?

My friends, pay very close attention to this chapter. This is your game-changer and the flip-switcher on your biz and life. Mean girls be gone! I'm talking about your committee, your crew, your tribe, whatever you want to call them; the people in your biz and life that make the difference. They are so important, I am dedicating an entire chapter to them. In fact, I could write a series of books around them. Yes, this subject is that important.

We need a series of people around us for various reasons: learning, inspiration, support, fun and even drive. People that complete you and help guide you to the next level of success. So why do we hang out with the Debbie-downers, the naysayers, and the general mojo-killers who take us to that bad, self-doubting place? Honestly, why do we do this? Seek out people that encourage you to be better than you thought you could be and break down that barrier that you put in front of yourself.

In my career, I believed my strongest successes came from planning and thinking strategically. I would assess opportunities in companies, develop a strategy and execute it with measurable results. I had a love for the drive of the corporate world with an entrepreneurial spirit. What I realized is that my strategies were only strategies on paper; it's how you inspire, influence, and impact other people that move you forward. We will explore the value of people and how without them, your success will more than likely be only lingering on the horizon, just out of reach. People will make the difference, and without them your Map will only stay on the drawing board.

Have you ever heard of any one individual, company, or empire making history or building greatness through the actions of just one person? From start to finish, do you think anyone has really ever made it on their own? No trick questions here. The answer is "no". It would be almost impossible to completely build anything on your own, and why would you attempt to do so? It would be more difficult and far less enjoyable. Making decisions, being creative, the heavy, the everything is tough to do on your own. You have heard the phrase, "It takes a village". Well, it does! It takes many people to get anything accomplished. Stop and think about it. In any important area of your life; from building a biz, raising a family, training for a marathon, moving from home to home, or making major biz or life decisions, it takes people supporting you and collaborating with others to drive you to your end goal. That's the message I'm sending,

People are your greatest asset.

Whether you're an entrepreneur or a CEO, have one employee or 1000 employees, work with a peer group, a team of consultants, or anything in between, you're in the people biz. You don't need to have a team of people or possess a fancy title to be in this biz. In my biz, I have one employee and a crew of consultants, vendors and service-based experts who keep my biz growing. I also have peers, advocates, mentors, collaborative partners, and clients. All of these people are of incredible value to me personally and to my biz. My crew has respect and trust in me, as I do for them. I hold all of the same roles as I just listed for other people as well. Collaborative to the core, my biz has succeeded because of the people I strategically assemble around me. Any journey, project or grand goal is so much more effective and enjoyable when you embrace the people in front of you, beside you, and behind you.

The right people make it happen.

What does this mean to you: "The right people make it happen"? Depending on your perspective, it can have very different meanings. It could mean you have a dialed-in team of people working through your strategies and knocking results out of the ballpark. It could be a support group who is supporting your state of mind to pursue your dreams or fight for what you believe in. The statement could mean you have a group of consultants who are so aligned with your vision, your biz continues to grow. It could also mean that you have a community of peers and professionals who are your advocates and make a difference in your life.

At different times within my career, I have had all of these things. You have heard the phrase "You turn into the people you associate with". In my opinion, this statement is true. The company you keep and the team or crew you have brought together can define who you are and what you will accomplish. Ask yourself:

Are you aligned with the right people?

Let me give you a few examples. A good amount of my clients came directly to me by referral, most from my crew. Some incredible ways to enhance my biz came from my crew. Some of the troubled paths I was close to taking were hindered because of my crew. See the pattern here? The peeps make the difference!

My crewmembers understand my vision, my planned accomplishments, my passion, my work, my strengths and challenges, and my values.

So, who believes in you? Who would go the extra mile for you? Who is advocating for you? I advocate for so many people every day who can not only turn out great work, but also have the heart for success, for biz, and for people. In any biz or personal relationship it's about having each other's back and helping each other out. However, if you do a good deed, you should not expect something in return. The message I am sending is that if you take care of people openly and with passion to see them succeed, they will be more likely do the same for you.

You are destined for greatness. Who will help you get there?

Within your company or your life, think of the people who would walk through fire to see your goals and dreams come to fruition. It should be clear by now that striving for any goal on your own is probably not the smartest idea. You need support beyond you. You need people to help to take on your mission, vision, drive your strategies to results. Your crew is a critical part of your Map.

Let's get started on determining how to form your crew. A strong crew would be ten people. There have been times I've had five people on my crew, and times that I would have 12 people. These are the people who support your biz moving forward and grow past even the highest of possibilities. The three questions to first ask are: What type of crewmember do I need? Where do you find them? And how do you meet with them? Let's explore.

1. What type of crewmembers do I need?

Your crewmembers can change starting at a quarterly to yearly basis, or can be rotating constantly. I have some crewmembers that will always be in the top three and others that will rotate in and out. It depends on where your biz focus is, the level of experts that you need, and influence you need as well as support. Every crewmember will form their own roll based on what you are working to accomplish. For example, when I am publishing my books, my publishing team is on my crew and is incredibly critical to the project's success. After the book is launched, my publishing team is off the radar and the next set of new members rotate in; maybe marketing and PR peeps. Your crew should be forever changing. My husband is number one on my crew and will forever remain there. He is my rock, my number one supporter, and also has a strong logic in biz. Call him the President of the KA Inc. crew!

The following list of people will give you an idea of what type of crewmembers you need to grow your biz. Keep in mind you may barely know them. They may even be a short-term consultant and will help flip the switch for you. Remember, this is your inner circle for biz growth.

Family and Friends   Virtual Assistant

Branding/Marketing Operations

Business Coach/Mentor	Services
Product Development	PR/Networking
Collaborative Partners	Joint Ventures
Employees	Consultants
CPA & Book keeper	Lawyer

There are a few constants that you should strive to always have on your crew:

Mentor: Everyone needs one! I have a mentor and even my mentor has a mentor. It is incredibly difficult to see inside your own biz. You must find a mentor based on the needs of your personal development and targeted biz growth.

Collaborative Partners: Everyone needs these too! These partners may service the same similar client or mirror each other in product or service offerings. They make fantastic referral partners and often are working to build similar types of businesses. Often times your collaborative partners believe in you or see more than you do in yourself. Collaborative partners will get you in front of the right people, and also to keep you on top of your game. You in turn will do the same for them.

2. Where do I find the crew members I need?

I have seen so many people search for the right people in all of the wrong places. When finding the right crew members, think and ask in relation to niche and expertise. You will find who you are looking for much quicker. For example, if you need a brand manager and you are a speaker, you would ask people if they knew any brand strategists or experts who specialize in working with speakers. Or you could just say I'm looking for someone who specializes in branding. See the difference? Be as specific as you can and know what you need before you go searching. It will save so much time!

Ask: Ask everyone you know for a referral of the exact type of person you are looking for.

Social Media: I have found many crewmembers through social media. Join groups and get involved in conversation.

Networking events: If your sweet spot client is a male ranging from 40-60 years in age and you are attending young women professional's events, you will not find potential clients or collaborative partners. When I go networking, I go looking for relationships, not clients. Biz is no longer transactional; it is relational. Keep in mind the types of events you are attending and the type of people there. Do they mirror what you are trying to accomplish?

Membership-based organizations or masterminds: Similar to networking. Are you joining groups that cater to executives when you need to collaborate and meet more people at ground level or vice versa? Are you spending your time at bar mixers when you should be at round tables in high-rise buildings? Think through your end result and what your biz needs are. That will determine the crew you need and where you are finding them. I have moved on from wonderful membership-based groups once I realized the type of people I needed to be in front of were not there. Think strategy, not quantity.

3. How do I meet with people?

Do you meet for coffee, lunch, drinks, or just jump on a call? How do you determine how to spend the right time with the right people? Be mindful with your time. Just because someone wants to have coffee with you doesn't mean you should. Maybe they are meant for a phone call.

First, identify what this person could potentially bring to the table by getting to know each other. Could they be a crewmember, potential client, a possible referral for a collaborative partner, or maybe you see no connection at all. How can this person best benefit your biz and build your network? What value will this person bring? You may not see a person as someone who could move anything in your biz, but maybe the two of you made a great connection and see a new friendship coming to life. That is fabulous too!

Here are some suggestions to determining how to meet with someone:

Sharing a meal: Crewmember,

Coffee or a drink: First meeting or have identified a connection.

Phone Call: Do not see a connection.

A special note on meetings; please do not intend to sell anything unless that was initially established when the appointment was made. No one appreciates being sold to! Make sure you're there to get to know them and understand the nature of their biz. Allow them to talk first and then you can better guide the conversation in the way that will be most effective for the both of you.

Let's determine your next steps how to find your crew. Below is a grid that will keep you on task, and help you find the right people to make your biz grow. Again, always work toward at least ten people.

Exercise

ESTABLISHING YOUR CREW GRID

1. <u>Name:</u> If you do not know who the name of this person is yet, write what their title or role would be. Example: Mentor, Marketing Expert

2. <u>Type:</u> What is the specific need? Example: Service, Collaborative Partner, Support

3. <u>Where to Find:</u> Where do you plan to search for this crewmember? Example: Social Media, networking, Referral

4. <u>Meeting Type:</u> What type of meeting will you have? Example: phone call, coffee, meal

5. <u>Scheduled:</u> Your planned meeting date

6. <u>On Crew:</u> Place a check mark when they are a part of your crew.

**Note, for all printable exercises within The Results Map book, go to KimberlyAlexanderInc.com

Establishing Your Crew

	Name	Type	Where to Find	Meeting Type	Scheduled	On Crew
1						
2						
3						
4						
5						
6						
7						
8						
9						
10						

You have determined types of crewmembers that you need, where to find them and how to meet with them. Now, equally as important, what do you do for them? Having a crew is not just about you and your biz, but how you form a lasting relationship and give back. What do you bring to the table? There are four simple words that will draw people to you. They are the Four I's: Identify, Inspire, Influence, and Impact

Identify

You have already worked through the last exercise to identify who or what type of person needs to be a part your crew. Who would advocate for you without even thinking twice? Who would want to see your strategy become a reality? How can you inspire, influence and impact others to see both of your visions come to fruition.

Inspire

The definition of inspire is to stimulate, motivate and encourage. This is sufficient, but I would add that to inspire is also to give someone a voice, and to empower them to be their best. If you inspire others, then they will inspire you. Every day I am inspired by those around me who share different perspectives, fresh ideas, and words of support. Have you ever met someone face to face, read their book, or watched their movie and found that the experience shook you to the core in a positive way? The first thing most people want to do is share their experience with the world and how it affected or even changed their life or biz. I am an avid fan of Brendon Burchard, author of *The Millionaire Messenger.* His book was as inspiring to me as I was building my company that I shared his book with at least 30 of my peers who I knew could use his advice. I was inspired to pay it forward. I wanted my friends, my advocates, and my crew to have the same experience I had and to see success. Imagine how your business could grow simply by inspiring others!

Influence

To guide and shape. Does your crew understand your vision? Do they get your mission and planned accomplishments? Do you understand theirs? Positive or negative, influence can affect your crew, whether it is as a small ripple in a pond or as a massive tsunami. Be mindful of who is influencing you and the crew that you can impact. You want to influence people for the greater good and to enhance experiences, learning, and positive outcomes.

Impact

To have a strong effect on someone or something. How are you growing personally and professionally from your association with your crew? What do they gain from you? When you think of someone who impacted your life professionally or personally, who immediately comes to mind? Remember the difference these people made in your life and think about how you can pay it forward to others. I have a few people on my crew that have been with me through ups, downs, transformations, and plans. The impact you have is a big reason why your crew will want to move mountains for you.

Exercise

Identify the people who make up your top ten crewmembers. Place a check mark under Inspire, Influence and Impact if you have made a difference to them in that area. If not, it's time to give back and pay it forward. Remember, your crew is a critical piece in building your Map.

YOUR CREW

Inspire	Influence	Impact
_____	_____	_____
_____	_____	_____
_____	_____	_____
_____	_____	_____
_____	_____	_____
_____	_____	_____
_____	_____	_____
_____	_____	_____
_____	_____	_____
_____	_____	_____

Ralph Waldo Emerson was a smart man. He understood the value of people and how sticking together could impact the world. He quotes,

"Most successful people I know make a difference in the lives they touch and bring a high level of value to the world."

My mom's favorite poem is written by this brilliant man and has become one of my favorites too. This poem is how I model the life I live, and how I cherish the people in it. Mom, this is for you.

Success

To laugh often and much. To win the respect of intelligent people and the affection of children.

To earn the appreciation of honest critics and endure the betrayal of false friends.

To appreciate beauty; to find the best in others.

To leave the world a bit better, whether by a healthy child, a garden patch or a redeemed social condition.

To know even one life has breathed easier because you have lived.

That is to have succeeded.

-Ralph Waldo Emerson

Kristie Keever
KristieKeever.com

When my son was first born, my journey started as a single parent. Let me clarify that I really mean single parent! The only other people that changed his diapers were the fabulous daycare staff who watched over him while I was working. I called on my Grandmother sometimes for help when she could, but she was older and saw my baby boy as my responsibility. So here I was, a single mom, with little support and his sole caregiver. He was my light during hard times.

I worked part-time for a print publication company and couldn't afford full-time daycare. I was in a tough position. I had to turn down my measly 25¢ quarterly raises in order to qualify for state supplemented day care. I felt stuck.

After payday and all of our living and personal expenses were covered I had $20 left to last me two weeks until I was paid again. Believe me when I say, one can really get creative with how to cut corners when you need to. When you have others who rely on you, there is always a way.

It was such a lonely time for me. I rarely ate out, had little to no friends, and aside from the pure joy of being his mama, I longed to share our lives with someone else who loved us. I knew we were both meant for more.

I wasn't making ends meet. My savings dwindled down to practically nothing and I thought to myself, "I have GOT to do something." I had this amazing career journey with loads of talent and skill sets under my belt. I just knew that our ability to survive was in my hands, and as my parents taught me, I could do anything that I set my mind to; I just had to figure out how. I knew there was more in this life that was meant for my son and me.

I didn't know many people in Denver at this time, having just relocated from Arizona, but I knew how to network and connect so just I started talking. I jumped on Craigslist to see if anyone needed miscellaneous sales or marketing help and I came across an ad that was the perfect fit. Alas, I was a freelancer. Little did I know that decision would change my life forever.

My first client, a Chiropractor, was an out-of-the-box thinker who was willing to try new things. As a result, we had a ton of fun working together on a variety of projects over the next couple of years. I also connected with my dentist for projects. My son loved the company and I loved the freedom of spending time with my son and working on my own time.

My biggest struggle was definitely fear. I constantly listened to the voices and doubts of others telling me how hard it was to work for yourself, and how there was no benefit or gain from owning your own business. I was told that I would never amount to anything. I knew different.

I knew that I was destined for more - destined for better. I've known this since I was 12 years old. That yearning and calling within me was there. I had a taste of employment freedom as a freelancer, and I knew that I had to shut out the negative naysayers, believe in myself, and just take that leap. It was the best thing I have ever done for myself. I did leap, but with walls as high as you can see, protecting me from any of those naysayers. What I didn't realize is I kept those walls up from the supporters too.

I have learned so many lessons. The biggest ah-ha moment for me during my journey was when I realized that the more you give of yourself the more you receive of others. Taking that leap into entrepreneurship is certainly the scariest thing I have ever done, but what I have learned is how to be authentic and transparent when giving of myself. I have been able to connect with my tribe, find my people, and live a blissful life.

As a branding strategist, I teach my clients to bring more of their authentic self into their brand and business. Their story is what allows them to find their tribe, connect with their audience, and have deeper, more fulfilling connections with people, both professionally and personally. What I didn't realize that while I was teaching this, I wasn't allowing this to happen in my own business and life.

I began to share more of myself, more of my story, and more of the journey and the people I met who have brought me where I am today. I started to see and feel the transformation in and around myself because of the connections I was making, the referrals I was receiving, and the conversations I was having with those around me.

The lesson is this: When you add transparency into your life and business, you allow yourself to be more relatable, likeable, and trustworthy to others. Let's face it; we all have a story - that is what makes us unique. There are pieces of our stories that others can relate to. Having similar experiences allows you to have a deeper, unspoken level of understanding with others.

When asked if I would go back and do anything differently, I wouldn't. These experiences are what makes my story and what make me unique. Things happen for a reason, and at the time they are supposed to. I am perfectly, imperfect me - right where I need to be in my journey.

Kristie is the Founder of Freshly Stated and KristieKeever.com. Kristie serves as a Brand Stylist and Strategist and is the CEO of her Digital Branding Agency.

Take Action. Grow Big!

People are your greatest asset.

» Your crew understands your purpose, the main fundamentals of your biz, who you serve, and what you are planning to accomplish. They know your weaknesses and strengths.

» Understand how to identify your crew.

Establish your crew with the Four I's:

» **Identify** the people in your top 10 crew.

» **Inspire** others and they will inspire you.

» **Influence** your crew through experiences, learning and positive outcomes.

» **Impact** your crew with value within your relationship.

Notes

_____

_____

_____

_____

_____

CHAPTER 6
THE DESTINATION

_____

*"What the world really needs are more alive and connected people who are
ready to thrive while helping others, in their own unique way."*
-Susannah Campora

The Results Map Fundamental: Strategy

Girlfriends, dreams take work. The more you work toward them the
easier the journey gets. If you don't have a plan you will fall into someone
else's. If you don't know where you're headed you will end up going in the
wrong direction. I dream and dream on a daily basis, and those dreams
never seem out of reach because of the strategy and plans I put to them.
How cool is that?

Transform your dreams into reality!

There are so many women in the world that have massive goals for
their biz. That is fabulous! What I find is that most women will start hiking
without any plan on how to get to the peak. Climbing a mountain takes a
strategy and it starts with the purpose of why you want to do it in the first
place.

So, where do you want your Map to take you and why do you want to
get there? There is not one person that would answer this question the
same way. This chapter will explore the foundation of your Map and your
purpose for building it

What you want.

Why you want it.

When you will get it.

Who will get you there.

All of these points will lay the groundwork for your Map. Without this understanding, all of the exercises and learning ahead will not matter. This chapter is where your Map begins.

Everyone has different ideals of which direction to take. The exciting thing is that business is always changing. What is important now may not matter in ten years.

Our outlook changes as we gain experience.

So what matters to you? Do you dream of what money can't buy? Is it status, having a family, recognition, a good title, time for yourself, love, or friendships? Or maybe you want what money *can* buy: a home, financial freedom, jewelry, travel, cars, apparel, a business, or entertainment? Maybe you want a little, or a lot, of both? Our desires are tempered by our life experience.

Understanding what you want in your biz is one of the most critical pieces to your Results Map.

There are the two exercises in this chapter that are designed to help you find what you want from your biz and your life.

Identifying what you want to accomplish both professionally and personally.

The four W's: Finding the what, why, when and who of your planned accomplishments.

Exercise

It's time to brainstorm! In the first exercise, fill in the lines below with what you want to accomplish. There is no time frame, no limits, and no minimums or maximums. Just shut down your brain and dream. For many, this first exercise was the most challenging because we have forgotten how to dream. Take a deep breath and take your time. You don't need to complete this in one sitting. Keep coming back and add onto it.

There are two types of planned accomplishments: Professional and Personal. First, brainstorm what you want to accomplish **professionally** on the first page. As Sarah Robbins would say, "Don't forget your daydreams." There is no accomplishment that is too little or too big. Challenge yourself to a minimum of ten planned accomplishments. Below are some listed examples to get your juices flowing:

Increase income	Bring in a partner
Get promoted	Develop an online course
Start a business	Launch a new program
Become a leader	Write a book

Note: Planned accomplishments are essentially strategic goals set to action. Words are powerful so use them wisely.

*Note, for all printable exercises within The Results Map book, go to KimberlyAlexanderInc.com

PLANNED PROFESSIONAL ACCOMPLISHMENTS

_____

_____

_____

_____

_____

_____

_____

_____

_____

_____

_____

_____

_____

_____

_____

_____

_____

_____

Next, brainstorm what you want to accomplish **personally** on the second page. Challenge yourself to a minimum of ten planned accomplishments.

Plant a garden	Get in shape
Learn a new hobby	Volunteer
Time with family	Paint the house
Organize the house	Journal every night

PLANNED PERSONAL ACCOMPLISHMENTS

_____

_____

_____

_____

_____

_____

_____

_____

_____

_____

_____

_____

_____

_____

_____

_____

_____

_____

_____

Well done! Now that you have your minimum of ten planned accomplishments, circle or highlight three planned accomplishments you want to achieve on the professional list and three on the personal list. Why only three you ask? Depending on the planned accomplishment, normally three accomplishments are the maximum of what most people can focus on at one time. You want to set yourself up for success and will have plenty of time to conquer the whole list, even if it keeps growing!

There are three critical questions to ask yourself when choosing your planned accomplishments:

Will it make a positive impact on my biz and life?

Will it make me proud?

Without it, will I be fulfilled?

Choose your planned accomplishments with your end results in mind!

Now that you have decided on your three planned accomplishments, both professional and personal, the next step is looking at the Four W's: What, Why, When and Who. The Four W's will continue to be your touchstone as you work your way through choice and change.

We will now identify what each "W" means and the reasoning and need behind each one.

What

Give me a woot, woot, you have just identified what you want to accomplish in the previous exercise, both within your professional and personal life. These are your planned accomplishments and they will forever be evolving and changing. Before I launched my career as a speaker, author, strategist, and mentor I had another biz I was building. I had big plans for what I wanted to accomplish. As I realized my life was taking a different direction, I had to be very strategic and "real" with my time. My planned accomplishments changed very quickly. Your planned accomplishments could alter should your overall strategy change.

Why

I could write an entire book on "The why". This area is so important because it is your purpose, your driver, and your inspiration that creates action. Your why will bring in the results. For example, I could say that my why for writing this book is to help rock star women reach their full potential…and then keep growing! This is true. However, it is also to make a living by following my passion and calling, be home with my family, and live the life I want to live. See the difference? You don't just need one reason to be your why. This requires deeper thinking in order to work toward the results you want in your biz. Your why is usually deeper than just one reason, so keep digging.

When

The "when" is the timeframe that your planned accomplishments are to be met. You may be able to forecast, but it may not be totally accurate until you work through a few more exercises. Some exercises in the coming chapters may alter your initial time frame, but answers will come. Be specific with a month and year. For example, don't write "in three months".

The more specific you can be, the more it will help you in planning your strategy.

As you embark on your journey, sooner or later, your end date may change . Learn from this. Some planned accomplishments are too aggressive. Many want to keep their time frame safe, and it ends up being too long. Challenge and stretch yourself to grow faster than you have while maintaining a realistic end date in mind. Again, with more clarity, determining time frames will get easier.

Who

We covered the importance and value of people and your crew in

Chapter Five. Let's review once more. What person or group of people will help get you to your planned accomplishments? Do you know who they are yet? It is important to know this because you may need to seek out that person or group for knowledge, connections, a service, or level of expertise. In this exercise you be able to pull from who you identified on your crew from the exercises in Chapter Five.

Exercise

Your next exercise will take some time. Determine the Four W's for your three planned accomplishments for both your professional and personal accomplishments. Take your time and don't race to fill in the blanks. This is not a task to be rushed, but an exercise that lays the foundation of your Map.

*Note, for all printable exercises within The Results Map book, go to KimberlyAlexanderInc.com

PROFESSIONAL: What	Why	When	Who

PERSONAL: What	Why	When	Who

Congratulations, way to go! You have just laid the foundation of your Map. Moving forward, choices will come clear and easier than ever before. You are on your way. I know this was a challenging exercise. You may be doing the happy dance right now or may be a little stunned and shocked of what was put on paper! Either way, sit for a minute and reflect on what you wrote down. You may feel that what you wrote cannot be achieved. Stop that negative thinking; *you can* and *will* do this!

The choice to change may come easy at some times and more difficult at others.

If you feel overwhelmed, go for a walk or call a friend to gain perspective. After you have been able to take a breath, come back to it. Dreaming and taking action past yourself is powerful. Remember, this process is a journey. Your answers will continue to come and believe that everything is possible.

Take on your journey with courage, determination and bliss!

Susannah Campora
susannahcampora.com

If I could go back and do anything differently, there is no question that I would. I would have started living my purpose in my 20's and let the fear go! I was on a roll in high school, yet in college I stopped expressing my true self and kept myself in a box, in the energy of mediocrity, safety, and numbness.

I have been through some dark times in my life where I felt uninspired, isolated, and disconnected from my true self and others. As an adult, I decided to leave these old stories behind and receive the support I needed. What really helped me to grow and thrive was my commitment to individual and group coaching, recovery, personal mentors, retreats, and seminars.

I learned the hard way that to distance myself from others because of my fear, excuses, insecurities, or silly, stubborn, "stand-alone superwoman" thinking was draining me and keeping me stuck and scattered in my personal and business life. This way of operating was not sustainable. I wanted both. I wanted success in both my personal life, as a mom, friend, partner, and success in my work, my purpose, my passions, and finances.

Most of these forms of support and growth required big commitments including time, money, and energy, but I felt there were key elements missing from them. As a busy mom of two and an entrepreneurial realtor for five years, I really needed individual development that was more personal, accessible, effective, affordable, and attractive for me. And I was on a mission to find it.

My own personal growth journey guided me to discover what my true-life purpose was. I remember seeing my private coach in action, helping me create real results in my life. I felt like I could do what she was doing, and I thought it was exactly what I was born to do. I jumped into a coaching certification program immediately, Institute for Professional Excellence in Coaching, and one year later, launched by own coaching business in January of 2014.

At the same time I launched my business, there was a call out for female leaders all over the world to guide women through a program. I jumped on the opportunity so that I could give the gift of a special women's group to others. However, little did I know at the time, that in this fun hobby, all my superpowers would be unleashed, my latent gifts expressed, and that I would discover the real reason why I was born! It ignited me to discover pure magic within myself and I was able to convey this magic very powerfully and effectively to the other women. I started using my own material: a delicate synthesis of my active intuition, and all the coaching skills and tools I received from my own personal experience, development, coaching school over the years. I intentionally and thoughtfully created the framework and elements of the experience.

What I didn't realize in my 20's was that we needed each other. We need each other on a real, deep level to support each other and to become better, happier people, full of life, love, and happiness. We need safe spaces to be vulnerable and bring about this type of growth. What I know now and teach others, is what the world really needs are more alive and connected people who are ready to thrive while helping others in their own unique way. And we cannot do it alone!

I have been an active entrepreneur for years, ever since I became a mom. Two high callings wrapped in one, whew!! When my first baby, Mia, was born in 2007 I was writing business plans, doing research, networking, and reading biz books, all while volunteering as moderator for a Denver Moms group of 3000. I also started my own moms groups, as well as volunteering in big community events. Then, in 2009, I launched my real estate career when I was pregnant with my second baby, Anthony. Through and through, a mommy go-getter and bringing home some cheddar for the family, all while chasing my dreams, and scheduling in my passions - in between diaper changing, movie dates with the husband, crazy evenings cooking dinner, and the sweet bedtime routines for my children.

No matter where I was at in my businesses, how old the kids were, or what was going on with my significant other and in personal life I have always needed support; support that really I needed, but did not seek out. Perhaps I didn't even know I needed it. I thought I could, and I tried, to do it all by myself. I'm too busy for anything else. Friends don't know what I'm going through. I need to focus on bringing home income. All of these excuses ensured that I did not express my best self in my work or at home.

When I finally stumbled upon circles of women who I could connect with deeper, who would listen, offer encouragement, and hearing a few of their own crazy, but found to be the norm, stories, I became rejuvenated, more confident, successful, and balanced. I found I could grow, expand, and love my life more easily. I felt normal and like I was not the only one. I started leaving the old stories behind, and stopped isolating myself. It was humbling for me to admit that I actually really needed others, and sometimes I still have a hard time with it. But I now see clearly. I really do need others, and I need to share my life with them, especially with other supportive women.

Susannah is a Life Coach and the Founder of Real Life Book Club. She coaches to get clear, get real and get going.

Take Action, Grow Big!

» Identifying and understanding what you want to accomplish both professionally and personally is one of the most critical pieces to your Results Map.

» When identifying your planned accomplishments ask yourself these three questions: Will it make a positive impact on my biz and life? Will it make me proud? Without it, will my life be fulfilled?

» Identify what you want. The why will drive you toward your goals; the when and who will get you there.

Notes

_____

_____

_____

_____

_____

CHAPTER 7
CHART YOUR COURSE

"Some people are lost in the fire and some people are built from it"
– Danelle Delgado

The Results Map Fundamental: Strategy

The base of the mountain is not where the good stuff happens. It's what's beyond the horizon that makes life worthwhile. Your crew and your strategy will get you to the top. You have laid the foundation for your success. The next phase of your Map will be determining how you will get there. It's time to chart your course. In this chapter, you will identify the right activities that will move you toward your planned accomplishments, while determining a time frame that makes sense for your biz and your life. Moving forward, you will take the perspective of mirroring your strategy to real time. Remember that "life in black and white" comment I made in Chapter One? Well, in this chapter, ladies, you will see what I mean.

Would you drive across the country without navigation, GPS, or even a paper map? Would you just get in your car and go without a plan? In my workshops and mentoring there is always that one person that will say, "Yes! Life is an adventure!"

But most people, they shake their heads, looking at me like I was crazy for even asking. So, let's say that the one "yes" person was headed from Los Angeles to New York. They may just head east and eventually, they would get there. But is it really that simple? There are different highways and bi-ways and scenic routes to take, but which route will get you to New York in the safest, quickest, and most efficient way possible? Will you arrive in the amount of time you need to get there?

Ladies think about it, could you plan your business this way? Probably not. Your business is no different than taking a road trip. You need planning and a strategy to get you to the end destination. Without a strategy, you can wind up even further off course, further away from your planned accomplishments, and you may not even realize it or see it.

One wrong decision or missed turn can take you off course.

Some of the activities you are engaged in now may be taking you away from your planned accomplishments. Assuming you have a current plan, you may be getting some projects done and landing some clients, but are you really growing your biz as quickly as you want to? Are you living the blissful, fabulous life you deserve?

Have you ever had a productive week scratching off the "to do" list tasks one by one? You put in 12-hour days, conducting meetings, attending meetings, working on projects and reports all the while thinking you were getting ahead. But when you assessed your accomplishments at the end of the week, you found that you really didn't complete anything? You thought you'd moved mountains, but really you'd only conquered the first hill. What happened?

This is common across most professionals' calendars. Tasks do get accomplished. But are they the tasks that build businesses, grow teams, make bonuses, and land accounts? We touch hundreds of things in our biz each week but never really move the needle.

Just because you are getting things done doesn't mean they are the most important things that you need to do.

I have seen this over and over again. The amount of time that you work toward a goal may not be as important as other things you're doing during that time.

You need to focus on the quality over the quantity of what you do.

It's time to work smarter, not harder. You may have grown at warp speed, but have hit a wall and can't determine why. Your current tactics will only take you so far. You need a strategic plan to chart your course based on what you want to accomplish, whether it be long or short term, or maybe even both. No detours, no scenic bi-ways; you have a business to build, a team to lead, and clients to serve. It's time to get on the expressway with your navigation guiding you to your destination.

Building your strategy may take you a day, a week, or a month. It's important to take your time with the materials covered in this chapter. The exercises that follow will hold an important piece of your Map. Give it the time and respect it needs to develop.

You are mapping out your future success.

Okay, it's time to build your strategy. I'm so excited for you! Let's start by talking about how you spend your time. There are two types of activities that we conduct on a daily basis: non-negotiable and negotiable activities. Identifying the differences between these types of activities is critical to your strategic plan, progress, and success.

Non-Negotiable Activities are high value, high urgency or high priority activities. They are critical activities that, if not completed, could hinder your planned accomplishments. They can be established weekly, monthly, or seasonally. Examples of Non-negotiable activities would be scheduled meetings, project deadlines, grocery shopping, and paying bills.

Negotiable Activities are low value, low urgency, or low priority. These activities, if not completed, would not hinder your planned accomplishments. These activities could be considered above and beyond required commitments or expectations. Examples of negotiable activities would be organizing your year-end taxes six months early, perfecting your work environment, or working on a project three weeks early when another project is due sooner.

A very important point to be mindful of is that non-negotiable and negotiable activities can vary in status based on the time of week, month, quarter, or year. When you are planning your strategy in the time frames above, take into account that a non-negotiable task in one month may become negotiable the next month, and vice versa.

Listed below are examples of what can change status from non-negotiable to negotiable:

Weekly: Meetings, presentations, networking

Monthly: Reports due, paying bills

Quarterly: Bonus reviews, planning

Yearly: Taxes, performance or biz reviews

Now that we have defined what non-negotiable and negotiable activities are, let's review the categories that your activities will fall under.

Professional: Planning, networking, marketing

Household: Grocery shopping, budget, chores

Relationships: Gatherings, activities, chatting

Individual: Hobbies, classes, YOU time

Rest: Reading, quiet time, sleep

Exercise

In this exercise you will be determining your strategy through a series of steps. Charting your activities, determining the time needed for each activity, identifying the non-negotiables, spot-checking your time to determine your strategy. Do not do two steps or a time or skip steps. Follow the process. You will be happy with what you see when completed.

<u>Step 1: Charting your activities</u>

On the charts below, list every activity that you complete within a **months'** time in each category. In the "professional" category, be sure to list a minimum of 25 activities. For example, if you list "meetings" make sure to include research time, planning, preparing, setting up, and conducting the meeting. That's five activities just for meetings! The same applies to strategic planning, networking, reviews, etc. For everything you list, think deeper into the smaller sub-activities you must finish in order to make the big activity a reality. Do not worry about the "time" column yet. Just list the activities.

**Note, for all printable exercises within The Results Map book, go to KimberlyAlexanderInc.com

Professional	Time
Total	

Household	Time
Total	

Relationships	Time
Total	

Individual	Time
Total	

Rest	Time
Total	

Step 2: Determine the time

Determine the time needed to complete each activity within a **week**. Using the same form, review the items listed and estimate how much time is needed per *average week*. If there is an activity that you only do once a month, include the total time. If there is an activity that you do weekly, include the time not for the entire month, but just for the average week. Below are some examples:

Professional: Networking	4.0 hours
Household: Shopping	2.0 hours
Relationships: Gatherings	2.5 hours
Individual: Exercising	5.0 hours
Rest: Sleeping	49.0 hours

Next, add the hours in each category and list that total at the bottom of each page. Then add the time from each category to get the total amount of time per week. Below are examples:

Professional:	120.0 hours
Household:	35.0 hours
Relationships:	25.0 hours
Individual:	15.0 hours
Rest:	49.0 hours
Total Time:	244.0 hours

Notice the number of total hours in the example. Remember, there are only **168 hours** in a week. For your average week, we are 76 hours over the actual amount of time that exists in one week. No wonder you are coming up short from your to-do list, you are simply out of time!

Some women may argue that although there are 244 hours on their list and only 168 hours in a week, they really are doing everything they listed. Yes, they may be touching everything on their list, but not in the amount of time they think they are putting into each category. I see this happen over and over again. You may be touching every part of your biz, but are you moving the needle on anything? My guess would be no. And on a side note, why are you touching everything and doing everything anyway? If you are, it's time to review Chapter Five again on your Crew and cross-check Chapter Six with the What, When, Why and Who Exercise. If you feel stuck here, it's time to call in the experts! Real time is real time and you must measure the value of your time and hiring out support. My first suggestion would be a Virtual or Administrative Assistant. They will do wonders for your biz and time. Bottom line…

It's time to get real with yourself in what it takes to build your biz

Some people may see similar results to the example above. Others may have time to add into their strategy. Regardless, this knowledge will get you your results. You are learning how to strategically filter what activities will move your business forward and what will hinder you from growth. But we are not done yet. We are moving onto the next phase of developing your strategy.

Step 3: Identify your non-negotiables.

Next, highlight every activity that, if not completed, would **hinder your biz** or your life. You will be identifying your non-negotiables. Now go back and add the time up again. Understand, there may be some projects or activities that are seasonal. Most businesses have their busy and slow seasons. There also may be different weeks where you are busier than others. For example, sales teams are busier at the end of the month, while training teams are normally busier at the beginning or the middle of the month. Now start highlighting! This is premier time working with activities that will move your biz forward. As important as everything seems right now, time is time and some tasks will need to go. It's OK, you can bring them back eventually, hire someone to complete them for you or never do them again.

Step 4: Spot-check your time

After you have highlighted your non-negotiables and calculated your new time, there are some questions to answer to spot check your progress:

Does your time add up to 168 hours for the week?

Do your highlighted activities align with your planned accomplishments and the Four W's – what, when, why and who established in Chapter Six?

Have you identified tasks that need to shuffle off of your plate and onto someone you need in your Crew – see Chapter Five

Do your highlighted activities align with the needs of your audience: your team, your clients, and your partners?

Stop and reflect on these questions. Are you currently focused on the right activities that will allow you what you want from your professional and personal life? Does your time reflect this? If you need to stop and go back for review, please do so. This is your biz and your life. Do not move forward with this book until you are comfortable with the outcome of this exercise.

Take the time to make it right!

Now that you see the amount of time non-negotiable activities take, you have two options:

Step 5: Determine your strategy

Option 1: You can **keep** the hours and time frames you have now, and work toward your planned accomplishments based on the needs of your biz and life.

Option 2: You can **adjust** the hours and time frames by altering your planned accomplishments based on the needs of your biz and life.

You must determine your planned accomplishment and the time it will take to get it. You can now see how much time you have outside of your non-negotiable tasks, as well as how much time you can afford to recommit to your planned accomplishments. You have identified what you want, why you want it, and who will get you there. What will come next is setting the boundaries of time that you are willing to work within.

Remember, your time should mirror your planned accomplishments

Whew! Take a breath. You have done incredible work! Feel proud in what you have done and how far you have come. Your Map is forming, so keep moving forward to make your accomplishments a reality.

Danelle Delgado
LifeIntended.org

The first 30 years of my life came fairly easily. I had achieved and became exactly what I had wanted. But that all changed the day I realized I had failed at the one thing I wanted to succeed in most. Marriage. I remember the moment my husband and I had our last real conversation. The moment I looked into his eyes and saw that he was no longer in love with me. Instead, his eyes were filled with anger and resentment. I hurt so deeply; I cried like I had never cried before. I remember thinking I had failed, feeling humiliated, embarrassed, mortified, and so utterly disappointed in myself. I had done exactly what my parents had done, which I never wanted to do. I had failed at love. I failed as a parent and was not going to be able to give my children a stable home, so I thought.

I looked to my mother for comfort, a shoulder to cry on and help, but to my utter shock, she snapped. I still have a hard time understanding why. My mother, with rage in her eyes, threw things across the living room and said the saddest and most lonely words to me. I was a disappointment to the whole family and was ruining everyone's lives. "You are making the wrong choice." She unleashed more rage than I had ever seen. I walked out of that room, a once trusted and comforting place, knowing she would never speak to me again if I stood up for myself, for what I needed, expected, and honored in a relationship. Nearly five years later, she has never spoken a word to me. Yet she remained by my ex-husband's side, doing what she felt I never did: shopping, cooking, cleaning, babysitting, ensuring he never had to feel the pain of losing me. She made sure that none of our mutual friends or family spoke to me. I lost so many in my life.

Alone in my apartment, with a new business taking hours of my time, I stopped and sat with my three children, my oldest at three years old and the twins at two years old. In the stillness of the room, snuggling, they asked me where we were going to sleep. Tears streamed down my face, I set up a tent. It was all I could think of! We pretended to camp for days until I could figure out what to do for furniture. I took them back and forth to their "dad's house" so that they could have what they needed. I wrote in a journal, "Today is the first day of the rest of my life", a quote my grandmother had always said to me. I wrote my wishes for my children, my goals for myself as a mother, and as a human being who wanted to make an impact. I promised myself to push myself harder than I could ever imagine. To start over, no family, no friends, not much of anything other than my broken heart and strong will to win. I would never allow anyone in this world to feel as defeated or incapable as I did at that very moment. I swore I would never again be here in this empty, broken place.

From there my business took off. I worked all hours of the day. I was in hundreds of meetings, business signings every month, and I created a beast of a thriving business. Although I had lost everything that had meant the most to me, I filled the voids with success in business and all the help I was giving others. After over a year of separation and moving into divorce, I knew my schedule and devotion to work was not going to bode well in court. I shut down my business and decided to start again where I could have more time for a new venture. I was hanging on by a thread.

Constantly tired and beaten down, I went to the doctor wondering what was wrong with me. After, the doctor called and wanted me to come in that day; I knew that couldn't be good. My kids and I trekked back to the doctor and I set them down to play. Looking up, the doctor's face was solemn. The words, "Cancer" and next step "radiation" exited her mouth. I said, "Excuse me? Look at the chart again please, you have me confused with someone else who hasn't had the last four years I have." Was I being punished for quitting and failing as a mom, wife, and daughter? Was this what my own mother had wished on me? Did I deserve this? Surely this could not be coming my way, this could not be my reality. I had built up such a wall to non-emotions after all I had been through. I refused to shed a tear, instead standing up and saying, "Well then let's get to it". With sheer confidence, I walked out of that room, saying, "I will beat this too."

I told only four people in my life about the diagnosis and was convinced I could handle it. Not until I was on the cool tile bathroom floor after treatment, extremely sick for hours on end did I think to myself, maybe this was not a wise choice. I looked at pictures on my phone of my kids and said, "I will beat this, and I will go and create a life that I am proud of." A life so big that even my greatest challengers, my family, will not be able to do anything, but celebrate the impact I am making in the world with me.

Through a series of events I decided to take a vacation by myself. My first day on the ship was glorious. Quiet, relaxing, with nothing I had to do. The next day I was ready to fill my schedule, work, connect, and keep all things business going. But there was no phone service, I had no friends, and I was forced to dig in. I had to look head on at where my life was at and which direction I was headed in the future. So there I sat, writing out ideas on Day Two of my journey.

Day Three was an excursion to Atlantis. An older woman leaned over and asked me if I was going to swim with the dolphins. I always thought that the idea would be freeing. So the woman looked at me, and with her strong British accent and said, "Well then, my darling, you are coming with me and we will do it together. We write our own songs, my lady." I said, "Well then, go we shall." There was so much meaning behind that moment in the ocean, being pushed through the water by a beautiful dolphin; the smile on my face in pictures says it all. I would be writing my own truths and my own rules from now on. I was ready to conquer the world.

The next day I awoke to a day in the Bahamas, on a private beach. I walked the entire island. I sat down with my feet in the sand, listening to the waves for nearly three hours, thinking, dreaming. I imagined how this new business was going to change lives and help people walk with a purpose and clear vision. I leaned over in the sand and wrote LIFE INTENDED. It would be a place where people can come to learn how to plan each step in advance and chart their course to success. A place where everyone can come and learn from the world's greats, the successful people who have walked before them, and would show them the way. THIS WAS IT! I shed some tears, ready to take my own journey of success for my children and for myself.

It took me years to realize that standing up for myself was the best decision I could have made. God rid me of judgment, conditional love, and anger that I had been raised with and replaced it with strength, refinement, and learning to stand up for myself. I was led to developing a core group of friends stronger than any family I have ever bonded with. I would never again pass judgement, love conditionally, or strive for an average life. I took a stand to love deeply, work fiercely, and always be an example of how I wanted my children to be raised.

I knew my new life was ready to unfold, with no boundaries, no judgment, and no fear of losing. I had everything to gain. This was our family's new purpose and journey, and we were going to make our mark on the world with it. This is my calling, and every day I give thanks for the fires that brought me to this place – my greatest life is being built every day.

Danelle is the Founder of Life Intended, a success-driven company for Entrepreneurs

Take Action. Grow Big!

List every activity you complete in a months' time.

» Assign an estimated time to each activity with the average week in mind.

» Identify your non-negotiable activities by highlighting or circling them. Add up the amount of time from only your non-negotiable activities and get the total. Does the number fall within 168 hours?

» Spot check your time. Does it fall in line with your planned accomplishments?

» Determine your strategy by choosing option one or two: keep or adjust.

Notes

_____

_____

_____

_____

_____

CHAPTER 8

DEFINING THOSE BOUNDARIES

_____

"Make your own rules; they will be far easier to follow."
– Denise Onofrey

The Results Map Fundamental: Strategy

Boundaries. They sound limiting, like they're going to keep you inside a box. However, with the right perspective and strategy, boundaries are actually quite the opposite. Sandra Yancey, Founder of ewomen Network, says, "Success is scheduled." Oh is she so wise!

Boundaries are simply protected time.

Time that no one can borrow, beg or steal from you, protected time that will see you through to your planned accomplishments and beyond. Boundaries will work for you, but they require extreme discipline. Making the right choices of what you protect and what you let go of will make a difference in the results you get.

In this chapter there are two things that will happen: First, you will continue to get real with your time. Second, you will put protected time into the strategy that you created in Chapter Seven. In previous chapters, you laid your foundation of your biz and life, and will now pull from that foundation for the rest of the book. The plan is for you to use these tools for the rest of your life. I have been using them for years and they always move me forward every time.

Think about what you have learned so far. These may be concepts that you have never thought about before. We just identified your strategy and focused on your non-negotiable activities. Stopping for a minute and thinking about what you want, why you want it, when you want it, and who will get you there is an incredible eye-opener. We talked about change and how making difficult choices will take you further than you had ever dreamed. We discussed fear and actually defining what could be holding you back and how to move forward. We explored defining purpose and clarity in order to determine your foundation. Lastly, we spoke about your crew: the people within your business and life that can collaborate with and support you in reaching your planned accomplishments. Continue to evaluate your strengths and passions based on what you learned about them in Chapters One through Six. Go back and review what you have learned again and again as you are working through the last few chapters. This learning will see you through to the end, I promise.

Gals, have you ever worked a tough week, ran yourself ragged, maybe ate three meals in your car three days in a row? Up at 5:00am, then in bed by 11:00pm and still waking up three times throughout the night, remembering what you didn't do? Or maybe you are so deep in reaction mode that you are planning your day three hours before it starts and not able to follow through on all of the great stuff you accomplished the day, maybe even week before? If someone else asks you for five minutes you just might crack. You look up at the end of the week and not a single project has been finished. Now you lose it and melt down. You worked hard, had a full calendar, attended and conducted meetings, and you still do not feel accomplished or that you have even made progress.

"Buried" was the word I used to use; I felt buried, exhausted, mentally drained, and felt like the "to-do" pile would never shrink. Does this sound familiar to you? Maybe only some of it sounds familiar, or maybe all of it does. You get the picture. I absolutely love this quote from Maya Angelou, "Do the best you can until you know better. Then when you know better, do better."

Ladies, it's time to do better.

Applying boundaries to your time is a powerful tool for addressing weeks like the one I just described. Getting real with your time is the difference in seeing increased results; what you plan to accomplish and the amount of time you dedicate to it will make it happen. Let's continue building your Map.

Boundaries and protected time are so important. There are four main reasons of why you should manage your boundaries well:

It will keep you on track with what you plan to accomplish.

It will enable you to be proactive instead of reactive.

It will enable you to adopt a sense of balance in all areas of your life.

It will help you to support healthy living.

Can I get an "Oh yes"? That is what I am talking about my friends! This is what boundaries will do for you! The four points above look pretty enticing to me. Allow them to resonate with you as we work through future chapters. First, achieving what you plan to accomplish will be easier for you if you protect your time with well-designed boundaries.

Again, your time should mirror your planned accomplishments.

I absolutely love this message and it really is true. Read it again, highlight it in your book: your time should mirror your planned accomplishments. Hundreds of thousands of people feel they are failing weekly, monthly, and yearly mainly because of how they manage their time. People may have the skills to achieve their planned accomplishments, but the amount of time they commit to working toward them simply doesn't match up. If your time and activities do not match up, you will not achieve what you have set out to do. Isn't it a relief realizing this? Your business strategies can now be formed into a black and white reality.

The second advantage of setting the correct boundaries is that you can be proactive rather than reactive with your time. Do you own your time or are you running behind it? Envision a train, a bus, or a taxi representing time and you are running after it trying to catch up. Have you ever felt like time is literally running away from you? It's time to stop being a passenger and become the driver.

Own your time. Control it. Get real with it. And you will see results.

One more example: My husband calls me the Voicemail Queen. Give me a crown any day, I am proud of that title. The reason why I love it, is because it is proof that I own my time. When my phone rings and I am in the middle of completing a project (and working within set boundaries to get it done), I will not pick up. Think about this: when you answer a call, the person on the opposite end now owns your time. Now, they may only ask you for five minutes, but wind up taking twenty. Or they might have a task or activity that they really need you to take on, but the time is lost and breaks up your productivity. This can happen day in and day out…and it does. All of this is avoidable. You call the shots with your time. Protect it with all of your might and see what rewards come as a result.

The third reason to set boundaries is for a sense of balance. Why would balance be so important in relation to achieving your planned accomplishments? Balance will bring more meaning to them and this will heighten every area of your life. Why make money, get promoted, start a new business, soar to new heights, but then have no one in your life to share it with? Balance will bring the perspective that what you are striving for is for the right reasons.

Balance does exist; it is simply a choice.

I have had many debates around this subject. Some experts claim that maintaining a work-life balance is not possible, almost as if the very thought is a myth in biz. In the current biz world, finding balance is no longer working nine to five, being home for dinner and off on weekends. The world of biz is very different now and women are playing on their own terms. The online industry has changed that for us. More than ever, women are working from home at all times of day and framing their role to cater to their life and values. If you want to get ahead, believe that you can take action and make choices in what balance looks like for you. One woman's sense of balance may vary from someone else's. It's about each individual woman's perspective of how they want to live their life and put protected time around it.

The fourth advantage is gained from maintaining good boundaries on your time and health. This is a big one, but it is not often spoken about in the biz world. A healthy lifestyle is critical to any successful person.

Your health has everything to do with your success.

Sleep, stress management, exercise, and even joy are all big factors in how you perform in your job. Sleep renews your mind and body keeping you sharp. Exercise relieves stress both mentally and physically; while joy brings you happiness and appreciation for all that you have in front of you. You owe it to yourself and your team to be on you're A-game. You will deliver more and enjoy it more along the way.

Protecting your time with boundaries will bring you lasting results. What it will require from you is discipline.

Exercise

The exercise you are about to explore will be easy for some and more challenging for others. You may have a perfect strategy in place, but realize that if you do not work through the tools and hold to your plan you will not get the results you desire.

My friends, it's time to get real with your time. You will be identifying your protected time within each category that we discussed in Chapter Seven. How much time will you invest into each area of your life? There are 168 hours in a week and 24 hours in a day; no more or less. Review the five categories within your life once again:

Professional: Projects, research networking, planning, meetings, driving

Household: Laundry, yard, grocery

shopping, post office, dry cleaning

 Relationships: Family, children, friends, partner

Individual: Exercise, hobbies,

volunteering, reading

Rest: Plan a minimum of seven hours of sleep per night

Step 1: Identify the hours you will invest into each category in a week.

Fill in the time in each box. The total number of hours must add up to 168 hours. Example: 60 hours for professional, eight hours for household.

First, identify the protected time and boundaries. If given a choice, how would you *choose* to live your life? These are your **future** boundaries that you will work to achieve.

Next, identify your **current** protected time and boundaries that you are currently working within.

*Note, for all printable exercises within

The Results Map book, go to KimberlyAlexanderInc.com

Future Boundaries

Professional	Household	Relationships	Individual	Sleep	Total
					168 hours

Current Boundaries

Professional	Household	Relationships	Individual	Sleep	Total
					168 hours

Time	Monday	Tuesday	Wednesday	Thursday	Friday	Saturday	Sunday
5:00							
6:00							
7:00							
8:00							
9:00							
10:00							
11:00							
12:00							
1:00							
2:00							
3:00							
4:00							
5:00							
6:00							
7:00							
8:00							
9:00							
10:00							

Be honest with yourself. Can you reach your planned accomplishments within these hours? Reference the non-negotiable exercise completed in Chapter Seven. Don't worry if you cannot answer this question yet, the answers will come.

Have you ever said, "I wish I had one more hour in the day or one more day in the week?" Gals, why are you asking for that extra time? Is it to do something that you love and enjoy, or to get something else done that you don't have enough time for?

Step 2: Establish blocks of protected time with each category.

Using the Monday through Sunday calendar, block out the time needed to fill the hours of each category.

Establish days in the week per category.

Establish hours within each day per category.

What days are you most effective within each non-negotiable activity?

Can you achieve your planned accomplishments with the above set boundaries?

Example: You work a full time job or own your own biz. You have decided in order to grow your biz you will need to learn a new skill. Your time investment to learn a new skill could look like:

15 hours a week, Monday – Saturday

Online program, 7:00pm – 9:00 pm

Homework on Saturdays, 10:00 am – 3:00 pm

This is an example of what you automatically need to add to your calendar and block out. You know you will need to be online at a certain time and to get homework done. If you double book yourself, you may miss a module or not get your projects or homework done. So note, if it is on your calendar, it will get done. Stick to your plan and practice discipline.

Now take a look at the parts of your calendar you blocked out based on the five categories of professional, household, relationships, individual, and rest. Reference your non-negotiable exercise from Chapter Seven.

Does the time needed to complete your non-negotiable activities fall in line with the boundaries you have set? What needs to be adjusted? Refer back to your options: can you keep things as they are, or do you need to increase the hours or move your planned accomplishments? Also note, you are blocking out non-negotiables. You do not need to account for every single task like taking a shower in the morning or brushing your teeth at night. No one person could hold to this type of regimented calendar, so please do not plan this way.

Let's stop and take a breath. How do you feel? Does your calendar look like what you thought it would? Can you fit it all in or are you out of time? Is your calendar so full you cannot fit in another hour? Did you add in more time at the beginning or end of the day before 5:00am and after 10:00pm? Do you want to make a change and live life according to the first set of hours you established?

Don't deflate. This is your life right in front of you; reality is staring you directly in the face. What you do with this information is entirely up to you. The good news is that the boundaries you want are within reach. You have been given the tools necessary to build the right strategy for how you want to build your biz and live the life you choose. Don't freeze! Make the choices necessary to get to the peak; it is waiting for you…

Denise Onofrey
DeniseOnofrey.com

I want other women to know how to make their own rules, buck the system, and to question status quo. The most important component of my journey to become an entrepreneur, to decide how I want the work part of my life to be, had everything to do with my personal life. I had always wanted to be a mother and have the "white picket fence" life. I mean, what else was I do to? I knew very few women from childhood who didn't have children. Of those women it had always been implied that they should be (or are openly) pitied. As a child, ever wondering, I could not understand why anyone would EVER choose not to have children if it meant that you were pitied or abnormal. In those inquisitive moments what I didn't know that for some it was a choice, as opposed to the curse everyone made it out to be.

So I went to Catholic school every day, and it seemed only seemed like I could be a nun, a teacher, or a woman (a.k.a. a mother) when I grew up. I wasn't so sure being a nun was my calling. The women who were both nuns and my teachers seemed to receive even more pity than the childless women did. Like most children, I had little exposure to options other than what I saw before me.

When I got to high school, I started to date other boys. It seemed highly admirable to be in a relationship and go to more than one prom with the same boy. Long-term relationships were the ideal after all. Would you like to know how many short-term relationships I've had? It was too many to count. I wasn't getting it "right" from the start.

Then I went to college, where I experienced freedom, choice, diversity, options, and wonder, wonder, wonder. I had one serious boyfriend in college whom I was sure was marriage material because what 20 year old male isn't? Years after our relationship ended, I was asked more than once why I broke up with him. It was because he got boring, because there was a cuter boy in my statistics class, because I was young.

I got married in my early 20's? It was what you did when you moved cross-country the minute you graduated from undergrad to be with a man. You enter the real world and become a wife. Somehow I had to make sense of my choice for others: "I moved and now I am getting married" (See? I know what I'm doing). The "M" word made everything better: first "man" and now "married".

In 2000, I woke up, sat up straight in bed and said out loud, "Oh my God". Sleeping next to one of the most generous, kind, loving, and understanding souls I ever knew, I had the realization that I could not be the mother of his children and he could not be the father of mine. Yes, I realize that was probably a part of the original deal in our marriage that I hadn't really thought through because getting married was a terrible, other-induced box I had to check. But I wanted to be real somehow. I had thought, from an early age that being partnered up, being a girlfriend, and then becoming a wife was how a girl becomes a real woman.

I left that marriage ungracefully, immaturely, painfully, and shamefully. I never looked back because I couldn't bear to see what I had done. I heard from others I nearly destroyed him and he wasn't handling it well. I was told my actions were "doing him dirty and wrong". I know... I was still getting it wrong. If I went back to him, where could I at least get some guidance? Where do I learn about being in relationships as opposed to only learning I should be in one?

So off I go without a man again. I had to fight tooth and nail to convince others I was making a good choice for myself, and my future children, and him. He was a great man, but I (we?) had made a mistake. Fast forward ten years: great men, great adventure. I fell in love with Colorado, and was working in a tough field to prove I had the grit and stick-to-itiveness that I didn't have for my marriage. I was still proving and striving for someone else, looking to legitimize myself.

In 2008, I woke up, sat up straight in bed and said out loud, "Oh my God". At 32 years old, in a decent relationship with yet another good man, I realized I might never be a mother. Remember those non-existent children I left my marriage for? Instead of panicking - that came later along with the grief and mourning of a motherhood I may never have - I sprang into action. I asked myself "what will you have wanted to accomplish when you look back on life as a grey haired, 80 year old woman?" That was a no-brainer: A therapist in private practice is the life I wanted to carve out for myself. Finally I had my own unchartered territory to navigate with my own rules and my own success. For the first time in my life failure was not an option. It was go time.

I had been too afraid to pursue life as a therapist any sooner, and to be honest, I remember telling myself, "I'll want to have a baby by the time I graduate – why even start? I'll be a mom soon." I started my graduate program in Counseling Psychology in the fall of 2008, six months after that wakeup call in the middle of the night. I paid keen attention to how to do this and do it well. It was my "baby". I decided to specialize in sex therapy in 2010 while still in the graduate program. I graduated in May of 2012.

Today, I have a kick-ass practice in Denver, CO and this is only the beginning. I serve who I want to work with, I'm surrounded by a brilliant support system to help me strive and thrive. In terms of motherhood I realized I have been mothering myself, as well as others all along. I needed to grow up, and learn the hard lessons about sex, love, and relationships, which I now pass on to others in the work I do.

I'm not sure I will ever be a mom with a baby of my own. Today, for me, a baby isn't a burning need or desire in my life. I often say what I love about babies is sometimes they show up in just the right place at just the right time.

So women: buck the system and question status quo. Have faith in yourself and always listen to your gut. If you make mistakes, don't make them your identity. Make your own rules; they will be far easier to follow.

Denise is the Founder of Anew Counseling and is a Certified Sex and Relationship Therapist.

Take Action. Grow Big!

Your time should mirror your planned accomplishments.

» Identify the boundaries that you currently work within and desire in the future.

» Reference the non-negotiable exercise from Chapter Seven and the planned accomplishment exercise (the Four W's) from Chapter Six. Do they mirror each other? What needs to be adjusted?

Notes

_____

_____

_____

_____

_____

CHAPTER 9
GETTING IT DONE

"I can do whatever I set my mind to and whatever I open my heart to receive."
-Katie Myers

The Results Map Fundamental: Results

Systems are methods used to effectively manage your Results Map. In this chapter you will learn how to establish processes from different timeframes to effectively manage your Map using daily, weekly, and monthly calendars.

Having systems in place can be a deal maker or a deal breaker. You know where you want to head, what boundaries and people you are willing to work with, and the right non-negotiable tasks to get you to your planned accomplishments. Without systems in place, everything you have worked so hard to strategically plan could just stay on the drawing board.

Now that you have all of the right information in front of you, it needs to be organized so you can start taking action. What will systems do for you?

Process and systems will bring you productivity, efficiency and results.

There are three levels in developing your systems for your Map:

Your Month: High-level, 30,000 foot view with low-level detail. Your month plan is your vision for the month (The Four W's, Chapter Six).

Your Week: Mid-level view with protected time (Boundaries, Chapter Eight). What your focus will be for the week.

Your Day: Low-level plan by the hour driven around non-negotiable activities (Strategy, Chapter Seven).

I have seen clients skip out on one or two systems, and when that happens there is a breakdown in detail. You risk losing sight of your planned accomplishments, sticking to your boundaries and making non-negotiable activities the priority. If you don't look high-level, you miss the message, the vision, the plan, and the end result you want to build. If you miss the mid-level, your boundaries, you will find yourself in reaction mode, out of the driver's seat and running to catch up. If you miss the low-level, or your daily planning, you are walking away from your strategy and non-negotiable activities.

It takes time to make it right.

You can set up your systems through your computer or phone, or even a planner from any office supply store, whichever you prefer. I manage my daily/hourly time through my phone and my week and month planning in a planner. Every woman has her preference on what tools to use.

Adopt a tool and use it!

Exercise

In this exercise you will set up your systems with a month, week, and day calendar

» <u>Month calendar:</u> High-level detail

» Set up your monthly calendar for one calendar year at a time.

» Add high-level events to your calendar that are currently planned. Example, company training or vacation

» Add tentative events to your calendar as they arise.

» You will review your month calendar at the start of every month. Some women prefer the last day of the month or the first day of the month.

» At the start of every month review monthly objectives: *events, vacation, and business trips.*

» Review your planned accomplishments to ensure they are reflected on your calendar and mirror the 4W's: what, when, why and who.

Example:

MON.	TUES.	WED.	THUR.	FRI.	SAT.	SUN.
30	31	1	2	3	4	5
Office	Comp Train	Comp Train	Field	Office	Kids Soccer	Open
6	7	8	9	10	11	12
Office	Board Meeting	Office	Field	Field	Kids Soccer	OFF
13	14	15	16	17	18	19
Office	Mgmt Meeting	Perf. Review	Perf Review	Office	OFF	OFF
20	21	22	23	24	25	26
Vaca.	Vaca.	Vaca.	Office	Office	Open	Open
27	28	29	30	31	1	2
Office	Field	Field	Open	Office	Open	Open

Week Calendar: Mid-level detail

Set up your weekly calendar for one calendar year at a time.

Add events to your calendar that are currently planned.

Add tentative events to your calendar as they arise, keeping in mind your established boundaries.

You will review your week calendar at the start of every week. Some women prefer Sunday night or Monday morning.

At the start of every week review your weekly objectives: *calls, meetings, and deadlines.*

Review your planned accomplishments to ensure they are reflected on your calendar and mirror your boundaries.

See example:

	Monday	Tuesday	Wednesday	Thursday	Friday
Time	1	2	3	4	5
9:00-9:30	Admin	Admin	Admin	Admin	Admin
9:30-10:30					
10:30-10:45	Planning	Field	Field	Field	Follow up
10:45-11:15					
11:15-11:45	Calls				
11:45-1:15	Lunch				Lunch
1:15-1:45	Calls				Projects
1:45-2:15		Lunch	Lunch	Lunch	
2:15-2:30					
2:30-3:00	Projects	Field	Field	Field	
3:00-3:30					
3:30-3:45					Reports
3:45-4:15	Email				
4:15-4:45	Social Media	Email	Email	Email	Email
4:45-5:00		Social Media	Social Media	Social Media	Social Media

Day Calendar: Low-level detail

Set up your daily calendar for one calendar year at a time.

Add events to your calendar that are currently planned.

Add tentative events to your calendar as they arise.

You will review your day calendar at the start of every day.

At the start of every day review daily objectives: *calls, emails, social media, and field appointments.*

Review your planned accomplishments to ensure they are reflected on your calendar and mirror your strategy as you did in Chapter Six.

Color-coding can be helpful in daily calendars as well.

See example:

Time	Monday 1	Tuesday 2	Wednesday 3	Thursday 4	Friday 5
9:00-9:30	Admin	Admin	Admin	Admin	Admin
9:30-10:30	email, reports	email, reports	email, reports	email, reports	email, reports
10:30-10:45	Planning	Field	Field	Field	Follow up
10:45-11:15	month, week	ABC acct	Blue Acct	Vendor 12	
11:15-11:45	Calls	DEF Acct	Red Acct	Vendor 10	
11:45-1:15	Lunch	XYZ Acct	Green Acct	Vendor 22	Lunch
1:15-1:45	Calls	Cold Call	Yellow Acct	Vendor 8	Projects
1:45-2:15	New biz	Lunch	Lunch	Lunch	Sales Planning
2:15-2:30	Existing biz				
2:30-3:00	Projects	National Acct	National Acct	Cold Call	
3:00-3:30	Proposals			10 potential	
3:30-3:45					Reports
3:45-4:15	Email				
4:15-4:45	Social Media	Email	Email	Email	Email
4:45-5:00		Social Media	Social Media	Social Media	Social Media

So what happens when the rest of the world doesn't follow your plan? You can have the perfect day, week, and month strategically planned and in place, but sometimes biz and life can get in the way. Things like no-shows, sickness, cancelled flights, and meetings running over can really mess up even the best plans. When different activities are cancelled, often times we feel elated at the thought of the gift of time, like it fell out of the sky with a big red bow. You've set your daily, weekly, and monthly calendars to reflect your planned accomplishments. You've taken those non-negotiable activities and put them to real time and you've set boundaries and strategies around them. Now what?

Stay in the protected time you have scheduled on your calendar. Stick to your plan!

I cannot stress this enough. If a potential client doesn't make a meeting, and your protected time includes new biz, you can follow up with other potential clients via phone or email. If your board member's plane was delayed, do some research on the industry, take a deep dive in analyzing trends, etc. Stay focused on the work that falls under the protected categories you established in earlier exercises. Stay disciplined and the rewards of owning your calendar and time will follow. Of course, adjustments will sometimes need to be made, but you can make these on a monthly, weekly, and daily basis. Always spot-check your calendar to ensure that it mirrors your planned accomplishments.

Now that we are all systems go, it's time to take action. Ladies, let's get your Map to work!

Katie Myers
CRconversations.com

I grew up in a very supportive and loving household. For as long as I can remember, I was told that I could do whatever I put my mind to. What that support meant to me is that whatever group, organization, or sport I found myself participating in, I had to be able to influence others. In every activity, I strived to be in a leadership role so I could have a say and an influence in how the activity was executed.

All girls go through some type of tragic drama with one another at some point in their lives. My drama started in middle school, where I lost my first group of friends. I found another lunch table and another group. It felt very strange feeling forced to develop new relationships so quickly. This is where the pattern began.

High school came around and it was some of the best days of my life. I was involved in all areas of the school from cheerleading, to keeping score at wrestling matches, to helping new freshmen get acquainted with the school. I sought out responsibilities and leadership positions because it allowed me to have a voice and a piece of control. Along with that voice and control came even more difficulty with relationships.

My senior year of high school became one of my biggest learning experiences. I lost the group of best friends that I had had for the last four years. A simple misunderstanding and miscommunication turned our relationship inside out and left me on the outskirts. I was crushed. I started to turn inward and really began to self-reflect on myself. Was it my fault? Were they right? I was so angry, broken-hearted, and desperate for resolution. The worst feeling of all was that I started to let their words become my own. I began to believe what they were saying and how they acted towards me. I finished out my senior year with an intense desire to attend college outside of my hometown and find my true friends. I needed to break the pattern.

I went to college about an hour and a half away from my hometown, with an open-mind and an open heart, hoping to find my real tribe. At orientation I found a group of girls who I immediately hit it off with. We were inseparable for the first six months of the year. And then another miscommunication and lack of feeling appreciated led to the fall-out and loss of two more girlfriends. The pattern continues on.

I ended up meeting my best friend, now of nine years. I finished my degree, started waiting tables, and loved it. I was able to connect with the customers and build a relationship with them even if it was just in the 60 - 90 minutes while they were eating. One night I waited on a couple and instantly made a connection. When I delivered their check they asked me if I would like to come and work for them. I sat down, right there, and said, "Tell me more!"

This couple owned an Insurance agency. They were some of the most compassionate, giving, and generous people I have ever met. I was beyond excited to work for them. I took my relationship skills from the service industry and applied them to my tasks in the insurance agency. I quickly moved into a sales position and was responsible for anything that touched the customer.

My relationship grew with my bosses and they quickly became like family. Sadly, they moved their business to Portland. I was asked to come, but decided to stay back in Denver. Our work relationship ceased, but we remained close friends and in contact over the next four years.

I found myself working for a life insurance company that primarily attracted millennials, like myself. Like typical Katie fashion, I quickly moved into a leadership role and began to build my own team of salespeople. I absolutely loved the freedom and the ability to build my own team. Communicating, inspiring, and motivating them became the most important aspect of my job. I loved engaging with them, showing them the ropes, and how to be successful.

My team and I were traveling across several states and meeting with incredible customers. An instant connection with customers was the key to establishing trust. My skills grew and I became very good at establishing a relationship with the client during the very first phone call. This attitude eventually leads me to a regional-level position, now conducting trainings and how to build relationships, referrals, and strong businesses. Not knowing it at the time, I found my calling, my purpose, and my pattern-breaker.

The travel was getting the better of me both emotionally and physically. I felt awful. I feared that my relationships with my best friend and my boyfriend would deteriorate. Why wouldn't they? I've lost so many people in my life, why not them too? I caught a virus and it forced me to stop everything and shut down for a few weeks. I will never forget having the conversation with Henry, my boyfriend, about what I was going to do next in my life. The job I had was very unhealthy for me. I felt stuck and lost, and felt, like many other millennials, like my college degree meant absolutely nothing.

I called my friends in Portland from the insurance agency. She wanted to start up a new business venture and asked me to be a part of it. We continued a conversation and, with full support from the people in my life, went in to business together as 50/50 partners. I quit my job and was so excited. I went all in and started to network, design processes, and go out and get customers. My partner and I met a few times a month to discuss how the company was growing. However, it very quickly became clear that we were at a crossroads and needed to make some changes. What happened next has been one of the most cataclysmic events in my life to date.

We had several conversations about what our roles would be. We agreed that speaking to a business lawyer to draw up the agreement would be in the best interest for both of us. I did just that and presented a proposal for restructure, as we had discussed. My whole world caved in when I received her response. She was enraged, hurt, disappointed, and threatened allegations that accused me of stealing the company. I had no idea on how to react. I ended up having to reciprocate with a lawyer to defend myself. I lost another friend and this one hit hard. The pattern continued.

I closed the company and was at a monumental crossroad. I sat with Henry one night with tears in my eyes and my hands shaking. I was terrified and excited as I shared how I had truly grown to love the entrepreneurial world after this small taste of business ownership. I loved meeting people, being a part of something that was my own creation, and being in control of my fate. Henry looked at me and said, "What you have been teaching and training in the insurance world, you should extend to the small business community". That sentence changed everything. I instantly felt a pull, my heart started beating faster, and something clicked. This was what I needed. This need for leadership, control, building relationships, and being a part of something great was the answer.

Two days after closing the partnership business, I opened Pure Communication LLC. I started that very day talking to people about how to build relationships with appreciation and communication. The universe had told me time and time again that those two components are things that I needed to share with the world. I had lost so many of my own relationships because of the lack of appreciation and communication. It was time to use my story and share it through my work.

I held my head high and went out into the world with my own identity and dream. My company evolved very quickly into a 100% relationship building company. I listened to my customers; I opened up my heart to accepting new relationships with new mentors. I kept my guard up, but remembered the two things that can make or break any relationship: communication and appreciation.

Going through my relationship challenges and looking back at the people I lost and the reasons our friendships fell apart, allows me to tell this story and look at it all as a series of gifts. I can do whatever I set my mind to and receive whatever I open my heart to. Every day I get to support my customers in communicating and appreciating their own Clients. If you think about it, where I have landed has been my life's work. No pattern necessary.

Katie is the Founder and CEO of CR Conversations, a customer retention and communications company.

Take Action. Grow Big!

» Establish your month calendar with your Four W's and planned accomplishments in mind.
» Establish your week calendar with your boundaries and protected time in mind.
» Establish your day calendar with your strategy, non-negotiable activities in mind.
» Stick with your plan and stay within your protected time.

Notes

_____

_____

_____

_____

_____

CHAPTER 10

ALL IN

_____

"If you have a vision and follow your passion you can take things as far as you want to go."
-Tina Gibbons

The Results Map Fundamental: Results

It's a chilly fall morning and I'm a bit down. My biz has hit a rough spot and I've been stewing in a big pot of emotion for hours. My head is pounding, I'm tense, tears streaming down my face from time to time. I've had dramatic highs and lows for months, and I'm tired. I hear my hubby get up so I grab my coffee and calculator and meet him on the couch for our typical Sunday morning chat. "Oh no", he proclaims as he sees me enter the room. "A calculator before 8:00am is never a good thing." We have a good laugh and then he very kindly asks what's up.

Poor guy, my big pot of emotion runneth over. I talk and talk and as he listens and listens. After my dissertation wraps up he looks me dead in the eye and says, "Kimberly, either you are all in, or get out. You know this is where you are meant to be. You know you can help so many people. But decide, right here, right now. Yes, you're in a tough time. Work through it. You always find a way."

It was like he had thrown a big bucket of cold water over my head. That day I woke up and owned my purpose. Owned what I'm here to do and nothing, and I mean nothing, would stop me. Ironically one month later, my biz had another breakthrough. I am forever thankful to my husband for that day. "All in" are two words I live by daily and pay it forward to the people in my life and biz.

It's time for you to decide. Are you all in? Are you ready to work through those tough days of fear, disbelief, stress, naysayers, losing clients, and falling short on revenue? The list could go on and on. When will your breakthrough come? It can be today, tomorrow, or even months from now. That is okay. Owning that you are all in will allow you a different state of mind to break through those barriers and enjoy what's on the other side. When you are having those tough days, pick this book back up and start reading. Then start doing!

Don't just live your biz and life; love your biz and life.

So you've done the hard work in this book and are maybe thinking, now what? It's time to make the choice to change, take action, and grow past your potential! In this chapter you will crosscheck all that you have learned to ensure that every exercise is in sync. Making even the smallest changes can require great discipline and behavior changes. Keep up the pace and keep going. Continue to work your Map to gain the results you desire, always remembering that your time should mirror your planned accomplishments. This is an exciting day…let's launch your Map.

Although my belief is that we never fully arrive you can always keep growing and evolving. Ladies, you have done just that and I applaud you for it. Bravo! You have worked through some challenging and maybe a little heart-wrenching work to get to this point.

Launch your Results Map with the right perspective.

We discussed fear, baggage, and have done exercises that require a lot of change. Change is much easier when you are crystal clear in what you want and understand the steps you need to take to get there. Sometimes we need to make tough choices and do the hard work to change. When you choose to make positive changes, even the smallest tweaks to your biz will show different results. Make tweaks along the way. Your biz will evolve as will your skill. You may need to go through The Results Map quarterly. As my business continues to grow, this is exactly what I do. When I start feeling overwhelmed, I rebuild and tweak my Map. Like the flip of a switch, I am back on track again and ready for the next challenge.

Discipline, discipline, discipline!

Many of these changes may feel uncomfortable at first and that is good. You need to break in new, lasting, and positive habits that will bring you the results you want. Discipline isn't easy. Jim Rohn says it so well: *"Discipline is the bridge between goals and accomplishment."* Set your mind to do and you will.

Have you ever seen a person going for a run in the middle of a snowstorm, the professional that returns every communication within twenty four hours, or the friend that skips dessert? Whether the smallest or toughest choices, these people practice discipline, and doing this will move you ahead when working through your Map. The results will come when you stick to it.

As you begin to put your Results Map to work, there are a few things I would like to review:

You are working to end less productive habits and create new, effective habits; this takes time.

Choices of change can be challenging. However, they will bring you great rewards.

Learn from your past to thrive in your present and future.

If you veer off of your plan, don't worry! Regroup, reassess, brush yourself off, and move forward. Don't get derailed by one setback. Learn and keep going.

The balance of this chapter will be a bullet-pointed refresher on the choices and changes that you have worked through over the course of this book. Brendon Burchard says, "The time to have the map is before you enter the woods." He is so right! We will review action steps needed in self-discovery, developing strategy, establishing boundaries, and building your systems. Every category will take an element of action required to see success. If action is not taken in every area, it can break down your Map, your process, and your results. Remember to take it one day at a time. If you fall, get right back up and brush yourself off. How do you eat an elephant? One bite at a time. The same can be said about your Map: take it one step at a time.

Self-Discovery Action Steps

» Understanding your fears and how they impact your choices in your biz and life are a critical step in taking the right actions. (Chapter Two)

» Whether you have experienced a win or lose, success or failure, victory or defeat, where is the lesson? Learn from them! (Chapter Three)

» Have you clearly defined your purpose? What does balance mean to you in your biz and life? (Chapter Four)

» Assemble your crew. First, whom do you need on your crew and where will you find them? Do you inspire, influence, and impact other people? Do they do the same for you? (Chapter Five)

Spot-Check: Do the four points above have a positive impact on your biz and life? Do they make you proud? Without them, would you be fulfilled? If not, we need to head back to the drawing board for a little more self-discovery. This piece of your map is the most critical. Perspective is the foundation of your success.

Strategy Action Steps

» Focus on the top three planned accomplishments in the professional category. (Chapter Six)

» Focus on the top three planned accomplishments in the personal category. (Chapter Six)

» From your three accomplishments, determine the Four W's: What, When, Why and Who. Are all of the boxes on your grid filled out? Do you need to do some research or network to find people to help get you to your planned accomplishment? (Chapter Six)

» Are the Four W's reflected in your calendar system? (Chapters Six and Nine)

» Identify your non-negotiable and negotiable activities. (Chapter Seven)

» Establish each non-negotiable activity with protected time. (Chapters Seven and Eight)

» Compare your non-negotiable activities to your planned accomplishments. Are they in sync? (Chapters Six and Seven)
» Based on a 168-hour week, does your strategy match your boundaries? (Chapters Seven and Eight)
» What adjustments will need to be made?
» Does your calendar mirror your planed accomplishments?

Spot-Check: Non-negotiable and negotiable activities can change status from week-to-week, month-to-month, or quarter-to-quarter.

Boundaries Action Steps

» Establish hours dedicated to professional, household, relationships, individual, and rest categories for both future and current boundaries. (Chapter Eight)
» Cross check: Do these hours match up to your non-negotiable activities? (Chapter Seven & Eight)
» Plan days ahead in the week per category. (Chapter Eight)
» Plan hours ahead within each day per category. (Chapter Eight)
» Own your protected time. (Chapter Eight)

Spot Check: Will you achieve your planned accomplishments with the above set boundaries and strategies?

Systems Action Steps

» Establish your month, week, and day calendars. (Chapter Nine)
» Review your calendar at the start of every month, every week, and every day. (Chapter Nine)
» Is your calendar achievable based on the strategies that you have created? (Chapters Seven and Nine)
» Is your calendar achievable based on the boundaries and protected times you have set? (Chapters Eight and Nine)
» What adjustments need to be made?

Spot-Check: Perspective, strategy and results.

Tina Gibbons
Tina Gibbons.com

I have always been a hard worker and I think that it often stems from a parent's encouragement and support. I had a paper route when I was 12 years old. I worked in retail and restaurants the very moment I could get a worker's permit. I figured out early on that it was great to pave your own way and not have to rely on others to get things done for you. It was nice to have my own money to buy the things I wanted. However, I couldn't have done it without my parents' support, car rides, and encouragement.

Flash forward through college and I am now married with a family and career. Early into my career, my mom had originally brought up direct sales as an option for me, specifically because she knew firsthand the potential it could bring me. My parent's had an incredible amount of success in the 1980's within the industry. She knew what I was earning in my corporate job, and there wasn't much left after childcare expense. Luckily, she helped watch our kids. Her friend was seeing incredible success with a direct selling jewelry company and really encouraged me to talk to her. At first I was very resistant; I didn't have a sales background and enjoyed working in Human Resources. Change is hard and it was tough for me to see myself walking away from the lucrative career that I was building. I had no idea the potential life and income it could bring me.

One of the things you don't want to miss as a parent is your children's "firsts". Their first word, first laugh, first step, first everything. While I was at work, my mom would send me pictures of her moments with them. It was bittersweet for me. I was so grateful that my children were with her and no one else, but it broke my heart that I was missing out on moments I felt I would never get back. We had to do what we needed to in order to make ends meet, and it was tough. I felt stuck. I can recall going to a bathroom stall at work, my eyes filling up with tears, because my mom had just sent me a photo of my son. Another moment missed. I had just missed him lift his head for the first time. Although I loved my job, it was then that I was prompted to give this direct selling job a try. I was determined not to miss any more of my children's "firsts" if I could help it.

I took the leap and joined a jewelry direct selling company to launch my own business. Within two years I was able to quit my job. It was a hard decision, but it made more sense to focus on my already growing business and to put my time and attention into what mattered to me. This opportunity even allowed my husband to stay home and help me market my business across the US.

I am now able to 100% work my schedule around my family. I don't miss many things. Our children know that though we will be at most things, we might miss some things, and they are okay with that. It's important that kids understand that. This it is a family business and I am able to be home because of the fact that I prioritize things. Coming to this agreement and understanding with your kids is a huge so they won't feel let down when business has to come first. Even with that, I am still around much more than if I was working for someone else. I recently saw a Facebook post from a friend; it was a picture of her sweet daughter getting a warm greeting from their dog. Her caption said, "Ah, these are the moments I can capture because I'm home when she gets off the bus." Boy, did that resonate with me!

When you are at the "growing" stage of your business you really do have to work hard and invest more. It can be hard on a family, but I think you have to put in your time. There is no quick and easy. Nothing replaces hard work and dedication. There are no shortcuts on that. Commitment and focus is key to building to success.

I am now a full-blown entrepreneur; it's in my soul. There are ups and downs with everything in life. What I do know is I love my time with my family. I love making a living from our own business and knowing there is always more to learn around the corner. I love the challenge of building and seeing a vision come to life. I love seeing how far I can take something and seeing people's lives change. I love watching my team grow and seeing them feel like they are unstoppable. If you have a vision and follow your passion you can take things as far as you want to go, but when times get tough (and they will) above all you cannot give up! You sometimes have to swim through the muddy waters to find the rainbow on the other side. Working hard is so worth where it can take you!

Tina is a Direct Selling Expert and a Leader at Lulu Avenue

What I have learned

I have learned that I am a forever student and that I still have a lot to learn!

Purpose is everything. It will drive you, fill you up, and never allow you to give up. It will see you to another day.

Relish in your successes, even the smallest of wins. They make you feel alive and instill your belief that you are meant to be right where you are.

Learn from you lessons. Often times it's the low points that have brought me some of my best solutions and made me stronger.

Sometimes it's necessary to blow off the afternoon and have coffee or wine with a friend, go for a run, play with the kids, or take a nap. If you're not "feeling it" nothing will happen. You will come back stronger the next day as the best version of who you are.

If you are not laughing every day, find a way. It fuels the soul.

Surround yourself with people that believe in you even more than you believe in yourself. Better yet, who challenge you to grow bigger than you can even imagine.

Don't let fear freeze you. Let it drive you with unbridled determination.

Seek out inspiration whether from a friend, mentor, book, workshop, or movie. Inspiration is all around you, just be open to looking for it.

Get your emotions out; they can get in the way. Laugh, cry, scream, throw a tantrum if necessary, and then laugh at yourself for doing it.

Tomorrow really is another day. Pick yourself up, brush yourself off, and jump back in.

When you need the time off, take it. The right people in front of you, beside you, and behind you will understand. If not, you're not surrounding yourself with the right people.

Get moving. Sweat, pump some iron, and get that heart racing! Your health will fuel you or set you back. Take good care of yourself. Some of my best ideas and clarity came from being breathless in hot yoga.

When you have a break through, celebrate it, own it, and be proud of it. You earned it.

If people try to bring you down, remember, it's "their stuff". Don't give power to the mean girls. If you are a mean girl, get the support you need to work on you instead of bringing down other.

Show up as your best. Leave your grump face at the door. If you can't turn it around, don't go.

Success doesn't come from luck, but from good, old fashioned, roll up your sleeves hard work. Some of the success I have today is from what I learned and worked for years ago.

Take time to reflect on what's possible, because anything is!

Believe in yourself every day.

Now ladies, what have you learned?

Your time is now and tomorrow is waiting for you. Greatness awaits, so let it out! Live your purpose, build the biz you believe you were meant to create and live the life you deserve. We get one chance at this crazy thing called life, so make it fabulous, make it authentic, make it you…

All in.

Take Action. Grow Big!

» Your time should mirror your planned accomplishments.

» Change can be challenging, but will bring great rewards.

» Discipline, discipline, discipline!

» Are your strategies, boundaries, and systems in sync with your planned accomplishments?

» Spot-check your progress with each step.

Notes

_____

_____

_____

_____

_____

CHAPTER 11
ONWARD

"Creating something bigger than yourself is 100% possible."
-Layne Alexander

The Results Map Fundamental: Results

"Be truthful, gentle and fearless"
-Gandhi

You can be anything you choose to be. I believe we never fully arrive. How boring would that be? We are here to learn lessons, win some, lose some, and continue our journey moving forward. So now that you have launched your Results Map, your job isn't done. It is important to monitor your progress on an on-going basis. I've mentioned this before that I take myself through The Results Map quarterly. Life changes, businesses grow and decrease, and everything has its season. We discussed in previous chapters about fear, change, and our past holding us back, as well as the need to find balance. Ladies, everything takes discipline. It is important to measure what is working well for you and what is not. Give each step time. I am never stressed or buried. I am excited for what each strategically planned day will bring me. I have a lot to conquer in my biz. Every activity that is a part of my biz has a planned time and day (or days) that I will work on them. Activities will get accomplished because it is in the plan, on the calendar, and has deliberate action behind it.

The following questions are guidelines for you to measure potential challenges, possibilities and improve results. You will want to review your self-discovery, strategies, boundaries, systems, and action steps in the first 30, 60 and 90 day-time frames to ensure they are working for you. After the first 90 days, and as your biz grows, you will want to review your Map quarterly. You may add new clients, a new team or staff members, new consultants or services, and maybe even new processes or revenue streams. You will want to incorporate these changes into your Map to continue to experience growth and success.

To help you, I've included journal pages to monitor your progress during your first 30, 60 and 90 days. I was never a person who wrote in a journal. As a child, I may have had a diary for a summer, but that's as far as I got. Two mentors that I highly respect had suggested that I journal once a week to write down my thoughts.

When referencing back, I couldn't believe the ideas I wrote down, the struggles and high points I experienced, and the learning and growing that transpired. Journaling does make a difference, so I am including it in your final exercise. I am now known as the journal junkie, and you will see the value in becoming one too. I want you to journal for 90 days so you can track your progress. Write down everything. Write down your highs and lows, your successes and failures, your emotion at the time, and the people in your biz and life. Include learning experiences, quotes, videos you've watched, and articles you've read. The answers will follow.

As a business owner, entrepreneur, professional, parent, friend, and community leader, you will have your highs and lows. Appreciate and be grateful for both.

For all of the roles you hold in your life, you need these experiences to be great.

"Success is not stumbled upon, or awarded, or given, or lucky. It is earned by passion, vision, consistency, a great plan, and a lot of hard work."
–Estee Lauder

As I bid farewell for now, I want to thank you for taking this journey.

Your biz, your relationships, your health, and your life will be better for it. Follow the fundamentals, tools, and processes to make the changes you need in order to get what you want. Exercise discipline, choose to make smart changes, fall in love with the process, and the results will come.

You have one life to live so make it your best. Enjoy the journey...

Layne Alexander
Registered Nurse

My mom entered my room, with tears in her eyes, and asked if I would go to my Dad's doctor's appointment the following day. I looked up and there we were, our family sitting in the waiting room, for my Dad to come out of his exploratory bronchoscopy. That day my world stopped. That day my life was forever changed. That day the doctor confirmed my worst fears. My Dad had stage 4 lung cancer.

I was working as an Account Executive in Arizona. It was my first "big girl" job out of college that challenged and taught me so much about myself. I was excited to start my life and loved where I was. Numb and emotionally wrecked from the news of Dad's diagnosis, I resigned from my job to spend time where it mattered. Within minutes that "big girl" job held no meaning. I knew that I wanted to spend every moment possible with my Dad, and working 40 to 60 hours a week would not allow me to do that. I started serving at a local restaurant, which allowed availability for every appointment, chemo day, and daddy/daughter time. I didn't know where I was going to go, but I was completely content with where I was.

About four months into my Dad's treatment, he and I went to lunch. I remember telling him, "Dad, I think I know what I want to do with my life." He gave me his big "OJ" smile. The smile that lights a room, makes you laugh and warms your heart. He said, "What, you don't want to be my assistant forever?" We laughed and I told him I wanted to be a nurse like Kristine, his chemo nurse. He smiled at me for a long time and then gave me his full support. God I love this man. In the coming months I thought about all of life's events that I would experience without him: when I get married, when I have kids, when life gets tough, and when life is celebrated. It started becoming real that I would never share these moments in time with him.

In light of my Dad's smile and wonderful support, I enrolled and I took prerequisite classes for the next year. I spent every moment I could with my Dad. It was the best year of my life.

My dad passed away June 1st, 2013. He lived with such joy and spirit, and passed it on contagiously to everyone he encountered. He was my biggest supporter, listener, jokester, and the first man who had my heart. It is impossible to tell my story without him because I would not be where I am today without him and his story.

Two weeks after my dad passed away, I got my acceptance in to Grand Canyon University's Accelerated Nursing Program. I spent the next 18 months working endless hours to officially become a nurse. The program was challenging in every aspect and pushed me to be the best I could be. I learned more than I could have ever imagined during my program, and held my dad in my heart and at the center of everything I did.

I graduated in December 2014, and can honestly say it was the proudest moment of my life. Walking across the stage, tears streamed down my face. I did it! I actually did it, and it was all thanks to God and my Dad. I am now employed at an incredible hospital working in the Emergency Department. The hospital itself is an organization I am beyond proud to be a part of. I go to work every day with a white lung cancer awareness ribbon on my badge to always remind myself to keep my patients close, make them feel safe and hopeful, include their family as much as possible, and to treat them like my Dad's nurses treated us: like one of their own. Death is indescribably hard, but having the motivation to work through it and create something bigger than yourself is 100% possible. Obviously I wish with all my heart that my Dad was physically still here, but I carry him in my heart every day.

Layne is a Registered Nurse in Arizona

Journaling Days 1-30

Have you defined your purpose?

Have you assembled at least ten people in your crew?

Are you working on your non-negotiable tasks first?

Do you own your protected time?

Are your systems in place and allowing you to stay within your strategies and boundaries?

Has organizing your time increased your efficiency and results?

Are you focused on the right people?

Have you gained control of your biz and life?

Are your planned accomplishments achievable?

What adjustments need to be made?

Journaling Days 1-30

_____

_____

_____

_____

_____

_____

_____

_____

_____

_____

_____

_____

_____

_____

_____

_____

_____

_____

_____

Journaling Days 1-30

_____

_____

_____

_____

_____

_____

_____

_____

_____

_____

_____

_____

_____

_____

_____

_____

_____

_____

_____

_____

_____

Journaling Days 1-30

_____

_____

_____

_____

_____

_____

_____

_____

_____

_____

_____

_____

_____

_____

_____

_____

_____

_____

_____

_____

_____

_____

_____

_____

Journaling Days 1-30

_____

_____

_____

_____

_____

_____

_____

_____

_____

_____

_____

_____

_____

_____

_____

_____

_____

_____

_____

_____

_____

_____

_____

Journaling Days 1-30

_____

_____

_____

_____

_____

_____

_____

_____

_____

_____

_____

_____

_____

_____

_____

_____

_____

_____

_____

_____

Journaling Days 31-60

Have you established balance?

Are you clear on what you need to accomplish?

Have you assembled at least ten people in your crew?

Are you working your non-negotiable tasks first?

Do you own your protected time?

Are your systems in place and allowing you to stay within your strategies and boundaries?

Has organizing your time increased your efficiency and results?

Are you focused on the right people?

Have you gained control of your biz and life?

Are your planned accomplishments achievable?

What adjustments need to be made?

Journaling Days 31-60

_____

_____

_____

_____

_____

_____

_____

_____

_____

_____

_____

_____

_____

_____

_____

_____

_____

_____

_____

Journaling Days 31-60

_____

_____

_____

_____

_____

_____

_____

_____

_____

_____

_____

_____

_____

_____

_____

_____

_____

_____

_____

_____

_____

_____

_____

Journaling Days 31-60

_____

_____

_____

_____

_____

_____

_____

_____

_____

_____

_____

_____

_____

_____

_____

_____

_____

_____

_____

_____

Journaling Days 31-60

_____

_____

_____

_____

_____

_____

_____

_____

_____

_____

_____

_____

_____

_____

_____

_____

_____

_____

_____

_____

_____

_____

Journaling Days 31-60

_____

_____

_____

_____

_____

_____

_____

_____

_____

_____

_____

_____

_____

_____

_____

_____

_____

_____

_____

_____

Journaling Days 61-90

Have you established balance?

Have you worked through your fears?

Have you assembled at least ten people in your crew?

Are you working your non-negotiable tasks first?

Do you own your protected time?

Are your systems in place and allowing you to stay within your strategies and boundaries?

Has organizing your time increased your efficiency and results?

Have you gained control of your business and your life?

Are your planned accomplishments achievable?

What adjustments need to be made?

Journaling Days 61-90

_____

_____

_____

_____

_____

_____

_____

_____

_____

_____

_____

_____

_____

_____

_____

_____

_____

_____

_____

_____

_____

_____

_____

Journaling Days 61-90

_____

_____

_____

_____

_____

_____

_____

_____

_____

_____

_____

_____

_____

_____

_____

_____

_____

_____

_____

_____

_____

_____

Journaling Days 61-90

_____

_____

_____

_____

_____

_____

_____

_____

_____

_____

_____

_____

_____

_____

_____

_____

_____

_____

_____

Journaling Days 61-90

_____

_____

_____

_____

_____

_____

_____

_____

_____

_____

_____

_____

_____

_____

_____

_____

_____

_____

_____

_____

_____

_____

Journaling Days 61-90

_____

_____

_____

_____

_____

_____

_____

_____

_____

_____

_____

_____

_____

_____

_____

_____

_____

_____

_____

Acknowledgements and BIG thanks

I am truly taken aback from the outreach and enthusiasm around this project. I have been forever inspired by the incredible women in this world, out there every day, making great things happen.

The Fabulous Women who shared their stories

Thank you, thank you, thank you for sharing your story. I have learned and grown so much from each and every one of you. You have touched and grown my heart many times over. I feel truly lucky to have been brought together from this project. You are all destined for greatness and beyond.

My hubby

JJ, my best friend and sweet love, this crazy, exciting and wonderful life we share is like no other. Thank you for your incredible partnership in life and in biz.

My Dad's

Oh how I miss you both. Losing you just one year from each other has stirred my soul. I ache for you both beyond measure. Dad C, your drive of being an Entrepreneur and passion for life is such a huge part of who I have become. Dad L, your kindness and continued belief in me set a strong foundation of always believing in possibilities. You are both forever in my heart. I will see you again someday.

My (Permanent) Crew

I truly could not have grown to where I am without you. You have made this journey so remarkable every step of the way. I am grateful to you all beyond words. Thank you for all that you are: JJ Alexander, Katie Myers, Kristie Keever, Michelle Jones, and Blake Alexander

My Family and Dear Friends

Thank you to everyone near and dear in my life for your continued love and support. It takes a level of energy being in my life and I am blessed that you are all along for the ride. It really is true that people make the difference. Love you all!

CPSIA information can be obtained
at www.ICGtesting.com
Printed in the USA
FSOW02n2350090816
23617FS